Printed and published in Great Britain by D. C. Thomson & Co., Ltd.,
155 Fleet Street, London EC4A 2HS. © D. C. THOMSON & CO., LTD., 1991

ISBN 0-85116-527-3

*(Certain stories do not appear exactly as originally published)*

# THE GOLDEN YEARS OF ADVENTURE STORIES

THE 1920s were transformed into the rip-roaring '20s by the arrival of three action-packed publications... ADVENTURE, ROVER and WIZARD. In those far off days, the exploits of early heroes like Telegraph Tim and Breakneck Billy were in words with an occasional illustration, a style of story-telling that was repeated when HOTSPUR and SKIPPER were launched a decade later.

The '30s were a boom time for adventure fiction, but when Europe was plunged into war in 1939 shortages and paper rationing soon followed. The result was issues carrying less pages and no longer appearing weekly. In 1941 SKIPPER ceased publication completely.

ROVER, WIZARD, ADVENTURE and HOTSPUR not only survived the hostilities, but emerged with a new type of story. Action, set during the Second World War, became one of the most consistently popular themes with readers.

Almost every home in Britain installed a television during the 1950s and to compete with this new technology the boys' papers began to include picture stories. VICTOR, an all-picture story paper, was introduced in 1961 and over the next few years the old-style stories were gradually phased out. The Wolf of Kabul, Wilson, Braddock and many other heroes gained a new generation of fans when their adventures were re-told in pictures.

During the '70s and '80s several new picture story papers were launched — SPIKE, BULLET, CHAMP and BUDDY among them, but WARLORD was by far the most successful and long-running of this new wave.

VICTOR, the glorious survivor of the adventure era, was given a new look in the spring of 1991. It now carries features on mountain bikes and the latest videos alongside its exciting serials and each Christmas VICTOR and HOTSPUR annuals are on sale.

There have been literally thousands of action-packed stories published during the last seventy years. This selection can only hint at the vast amount of material created during... the golden years of adventure stories.

## SCHOOLDAYS

Red Circle School in the 1940s and Kingsway Comp in the '80s have only one thing in common ... you'll love reading about both of them!

## SPORT

He liked the game so much he bought the team! Meet Gorgeous Gus, millionaire and ace striker ... then get hooked on our angling story Cast Hook and Strike.

## THE RUNNERS

Two athletic stories to leave you breathless and gasping for more. Alf Tupper and Wilson head for the winning tape in very different races.

## WAR

Fly with Sergeant Pilot Braddock on a daring raid ... then slip behind enemy lines with Lord Peter Flint and the mysterious masked figures whose battle cry is 'V For Vengeance'.

## THE GREAT ADVENTURE STORIES

Thrill-a-minute! Morgyn The Mighty, Africa's strongest man, faces up to a herd of wild elephants ... The Wolf of Kabul, and Chung, his faithful servant, battle heavily-armed rebel tribesmen. Chung's only weapon is a cricket bat ... and the Hairy Sheriff makes a monkey of his human opponents in a Wild West tale that mixes thrills and laughs.

# The RUNNER

The RUNNER

AWARDED TO SERGEANT
WILLIAM WILSON, 18th
YORKSHIRE MILITIA, FOR
HONOURABLE SERVICE
1799

Wilson, The Man In Black, couldn't have timed his dramatic arrival better if he'd tried. In 1943, the country was at war with Germany and a British sporting victory, even in the pages of *WIZARD*, was a morale booster. Any champion runner would have been hailed as a hero, but a mystery man who'd lived rough on the Yorkshire Moors for an incredible 150 years was the stuff legends are made of.

# The RUNNERS The RUN

Alf Tupper, known to his legion of young fans as 'Tough Of The Track' didn't heed the scoffs of his toffee-nosed opponents. In fact, Alf did his share of scoffing — usually a fish supper, straight from the newspaper. He reckoned nothing set him up better for a big race, and Alf had a pile of trophies to prove it. The Tupper tale overleaf introduced readers of *ROVER* to 'The Tough' in 1949.

THE TOUGH OF THE TRACK

WHEN the runners in the 440 Yards were called for at the Greystone Harriers' sports, Alf Tupper pulled off his ragged jacket, tossed it on to the ground and trotted to the starting line.

"Hello," he said to Vic Mason, the Harriers' best quarter-miler.

Mason's nod was curt. No fashion-plate athlete was Alf. He would never have been chosen to carry the Flame at the Olympic Games. His hair wanted cutting and he was wearing an old under-vest as a singlet. His hands were blackened and hard as a result of his job in Ike Smith's two-man welding shop under a railway arch in the town.

Mr Jack Pearce, the Starter, loaded his pistol. It was just an evening meeting and only members of the Harriers were competing. Alf, who was nearly nineteen, had been a member for about three weeks. It had taken him the best part of the winter to scrape together the half-guinea subscription, for he was apprenticed to Ike Smith and his wages only came to twenty-five shillings a week. Of this sum, a big cut went to his Aunt Meg with whom he stayed down Anchor Alley.

"On your marks!" Pearce shouted.

Alf dug himself a starting hole. He was next to Mason, and three other runners were outside him on the rather rough cinder track.

The Starter raised the gun.

"Get set!" he shouted.

Mason sprang away and an instant later the pistol banged. A shout broke from Alf, but the Starter did not call a false start.

"You ain't getting away with that, Mason!" yelled Alf, and put his foot between Mason's striding legs.

Mason stumbled and crashed to the cinders. Officials shouted and ran towards the scene.

With fury on his face, Mason scrambled up.

"You dirty dog!" he shouted.

"You're the dirty dog!" snarled Alf.

"You jumped the blooming gun!"

Mason swung at him. Alf ducked and then smashed his fist against the other runner's nose.

Bob Richards, the honorary secretary, grabbed Alf's arm and pulled him back.

"None of that!" he snapped angrily.

Alf pointed at the Starter.

"He's a bald-headed, old twister," he growled. "He knew it was a false start, but he never fetched Mason back."

Mr Ken Roberts, an old runner and now the chairman of the club, hurried to the spot.

"Get off the track, Tupper!" he rapped out. "Get off! You're out of the race."

"Yes, and I can tell you that your behaviour will be considered by the Committee," added Richards, curtly.

Alf looked at the Starter and muttered something out of the corner of his mouth as he walked off the track.

Mason, surrounded by sympathetic officials, wiped a smear of blood from his nose and said he was ready to go. Alf stood sullenly as the Starter told the four runners to get on their marks.

"Get set!"

At the bang of the pistol, Mason and the other runners burst away from the line. Shouts broke out from the indignant officials as Alf, on the grass on the outer edge of the track, went into his stride and started as well.

"What's his idea?" exclaimed Roberts. "Silly fool!"

There were jeers as well as indignant remarks for, outside there, Alf had at least twenty yards further to run than Mason on the inside of the track.

With Alf plugging along on his own, Mason cut away from the other competitors. With an easy, balanced stride, his arms moving smoothly, he padded along. Alf looked hunched, for he ducked his head down as if he had to butt his way along and his arm movements were jerky.

At halfway, Mason had a five-yards lead on the next man — but Alf was level with him on the outside. The Harriers' crack runner sped on. Alf was not to be shaken off. He plugged along and he was still there, thirty yards from the tape.

Mason cut loose and spurted. He worked up his finishing dash and went all out for the tape. He was two strides away, when a figure swerved on to the track and carried the tape away round his chest.

It was Alf round whom the tape was dangling. He turned and his lips shaped for a razzberry. This he delivered with loud effect.

Then, snatching up his jacket, he stamped away.

Sparks were flying in the dark welding shop a couple of afternoons later, as, wearing goggles and gloves, Alf worked on a cracked cylinder block.

Ike Smith looked up.

"Get your bike and take the radiator along to Granton Hall," he grunted.

Alf stared at the big hot-water radiator that had come in for a cracked joint to be welded.

"How am I going to hang that on my bike?" he snarled.

"Take the bloomin' handcart then," said his employer.

With the wheels creaking and the radiator clanging, Alf shoved the handcart down the cobbled alleyway to the street. Then he started on the mile-long journey to the suburbs.

On a neat board at the entrance to the drive was the notice, "Granton Hall Athletics Centre". Alf pushed his handcart on up the drive towards the big house. He noticed that the flags were flying and a crowd had gathered in front of the terrace. A man — Alf did not know he was the Mayor of Greystone — was making a speech.

The din kicked up by Alf's vehicle caused people to turn and signal him to stop. He pulled up. He had no idea that his errand would clash with the opening ceremony of the new institution.

The Mayor's voice boomed out in his concluding words.

"It is particularly gratifying," he said, "that the Warden is to be Commander Harold Churcher, who was a member of the British team that won an Olympic Games relay race. I am now going to ask him to tell us his plans for the Granton Hall Athletics Centre."

"Gosh! Commander Churcher!" muttered Alf. "I never knew he was coming here!"

Commander Churcher, an extremely fit-looking man of about forty, looked down at his audience from the terrace. He was bare-headed, and wearing a dark red blazer and white flannels.

"If I were to ask you why Great Britain did not fare better in the recent Olympic Games I think you might possibly reply that our athletes did not have behind them the organisation and the coaching facilities enjoyed by competitors from other countries," he said. "It is because some of us feel so strongly about this that we are today opening Granton Hall Athletics Centre. This centre, we hope, will become a permanent fixture in the athletic life of the country — dedicated to the discovery and development of the promising material in which this country abounds."

Churcher paused to let his words sink in.

Churcher then invited the visitors to split up into parties for conducted tours of the new establishment. Alf abandoned his handcart and attached himself to a group of people who had Vince Rogers as their guide.

First of all, he took them into the field. The oval track, he said, was equal in quality to that which had gained so many compliments at Wembley. The closely-sown turf inside the oval was, he said, good enough for championship lawn tennis. He showed them the jumping pits and then took them into the box where the timing equipment was installed.

Then he took his party back across the field to the gymnasium that was fitted up with every modern appliance.

He took them on into the cinema and then into the lecture hall. He showed them the massage rooms and the heat therapy department.

At the kitchen door, he handed them on to Doctor Bryant, the medical officer and diet expert of the establishment. When the latter started to talk about calories and vitamins, Alf ceased to be interested and slipped out to fetch the hand-cart and push it round to the back door.

He was just going to unload the radiator when a fellow of about his own age, wearing a dark red blazer and flannel trousers, hurried across the courtyard.

Alf blinked.

"Howard, what are you doing here?" he exclaimed, for Howard Potter had been at the same school as Alf.

Howard spoke loftily.

"I'm on the staff," he said.

"What's your job — cleaning out the drains?" asked Alf.

"I am in the office," retorted Howard.

"Chase me, you don't half look a sight in them togs," growled Alf. "Who parted your hair for you?"

"You'd like to be here," Howard said indignantly.

"Me?" Alf uttered a sarcastic laugh. "I wouldn't be seen dead in them togs. I ain't no cissy."

Turning his back on Howard Potter, Alf started to unload the radiator.

NEXT morning Alf, half-asleep, heard the stairs creak under Aunt Meg's weight. Their place in Anchor Alley had one room up and one down. His bed was a mattress on the kitchen floor.

"Get up, you lazy young hound," bawled Aunt Meg, a big, brawny woman, with her hair hanging over her red, bad-tempered face. "Get up!"

She padded across the dirty flagstones in her bare feet and started to poke at the ashes under the copper. She took in washing and the continuous steam in the air kept the peeling walls running with water.

Alf stood up. He rolled up the mattress and pushed it under the table. He had slept in his shirt and trousers. Now he stuck his feet in his boots, picked up a bucket and went out to fill it at the tap down the yard.

He had a swill while he was out there. Then he took the bucket back into the

house. Aunt Meg had made the tea. She took half a loaf and a greasy package of "marge" from a cupboard and put them on the dirty sheet of newspaper that served for a tablecloth.

Alf was eating a thick piece of bread when there was a tap at the door. When he opened it, he was surprised to see the postman holding out a letter.

The letter bore the heading of the Greystone Harriers. Alf's face was fierce as he read —

"I am directed by the Committee to instruct you to return your membership card herewith. Your violent behaviour was not in keeping with the standards expected of a Harrier, and your membership is hereby cancelled. Yours faithfully, Bob Richards, Hon. Secretary."

With a growl, Alf crunched up the letter and slung it into the fire. The loss of his membership meant that now he had nowhere to do his training. The Harriers were the only local athletic club.

Aunt Meg scowled at her nephew.

"Going to hang about here all morning?" she shouted through the thickening steam. "Get along to your work!"

Alf hacked himself a slice off the loaf, spread it with margarine, and tore a strip off the "tablecloth" to wrap it up in. Then he went off to the workshop, riding the ramshackle bike he had had for years and which had been old when he got it off a rubbish heap.

There was work to do on some angle-pipes for the Granton Hall heating system. He and Ike Smith finished that job in the middle of the morning and the boss told him to take them along.

Alf tied the pipes to the handlebars and pedalled away to Granton Hall. Over the hedge, he saw that running and jumping was going on in the field. According to a paragraph he had seen in Ike Smith's newspaper, twelve athletes were now staying permanently at the Hall, while another twenty had arrived on a fortnight's course.

He had just turned into the drive when the boom of loudspeakers startled

him and caused him to swerve.

"Will everybody come to the cinema please," requested the announcer. "Please assemble in the cinema."

Alf put a leg out to regain his balance and pulled up. From all directions, coaches and students were cantering towards the cinema.

As he stood astride the bike in the drive, he looked towards the now deserted field and at the reddish track curving away round the closely-mown grass.

Alf's eyes flashed.

"Nuts to the Harriers!" he muttered, as he leaned the bike against a tree. "Let 'em keep their blooming cinders!"

He pushed his way through the bushes lining the drive and vaulted the fence into the field. Off came his jacket and then his boots. There were so many holes in his socks that he was practically in his bare feet. He trotted on to the track and sampled the hard, true surface with a toe.

Off he went round the track, warming up and taking it easily. He carried on steadily and was breathing easily when he finished the quarter-mile circuit.

He did two laps of alternate jogging and sprinting. He had a breather and felt fine. Turning on to the grass, he ran towards one of the long-jump pits, worked up speed, took off and flopped down opposite the 21 ft. mark. The bar on the high jump frame had been left on the pegs at 5 ft. 10 in.

"I reckon I can jump that," sniffed Alf — and then did it.

A javelin had been left about. Alf picked it up. He had never had a javelin in his hand before, but that did not stop him swinging it back and having a throw.

He was watching it fly away, when an angry voice rang out.

Howard Potter came running towards him.

"Get out of here!" he shouted. "Get out, you cheeky dog!"

"Did you call me a cheeky dog?" snarled Alf.

"You heard me!" said the bigger youth. "Oh!"

Alf swung out with his fist and his knuckles clipped Howard's chin.

"All right, you've asked for it!" Potter exclaimed. "If you want a good hiding, you can have it!"

Alf made a rush at Howard. He left himself wide open to anyone with any knowledge of boxing, and the punch he received cut his lip.

Howard was strong. He had some skill as a boxer and was being coached by Bob Ellis. He hit Alf on the chin and sent him down on his knees.

In a moment Alf was up and going for Howard again. He ran his chin into a straight left and dropped. He scrambled up. Howard darted in and again put him down.

Commander Churcher ran into the field shouting.

"Stop it! Stop it!" he exclaimed.

Alf stared round and had a blurred glimpse of Churcher striding towards him. He dodged away, snatched up his boots and jacket and bolted.

ABOUT a week later, Commander Churcher lectured on athletic fitness in the cinema. At the end of his talk he asked Clem Gatacre to come up to his office.

"I've one or two things to talk about," said the Commander. "We have been invited, by the way, to enter a team in the Town Sports, and, though it's small stuff, I think we should stay on friendly terms with our neighbours."

"Yes, sir, we don't want to appear stand-offish," agreed Gatacre. "After all, we — "

He was interrupted by the Commander, who had glanced out of the window.

"Well I'm blowed, he's at it again!" the Commander snapped.

Gatacre hurried to the window. It gave a view of the field. There, jogging round the track, was a lone runner.

"Go and catch him!" exclaimed the Commander. "It's that fellow from the town again."

Gatacre nodded and slipped out of the room. Churcher remained at the window. He watched Alf lap the track — and then saw Gatacre enter the field.

The Commander saw Alf glance over his shoulder, snatch up his jacket and run towards the gate on the far side of the field.

Churcher moved towards his desk and was engaged on the phone for a couple of minutes.

The door opened. Gatacre, red in the face, walked in breathlessly.

"Well, where is he?" snapped Churcher.

Gatacre looked decidedly shamefaced.

"I couldn't catch him," he said.

"You couldn't catch him?" gasped Churcher.

"Of course, I wasn't in running togs," began Gatacre.

"Neither was he!" retorted the Commander. "You couldn't catch him, you said?"

"He jumped the gate," replied Gatacre. "His bike was waiting and he was off like a shot."

"Umphm, surprising!" said Churcher. "Well, next time he comes we'll make sure he doesn't have the chance to run away."

ON Friday night, Aunt Meg's voice rang out angrily in the kitchen. Her eyes were fierce as she looked at the money Alf had just handed over. It was the day he got his wages.

"Where's the other half-dollar?" she demanded. "There's only a quid here out of your twenty-five bob."

Alf shifted round to the other side of the table.

"I want five bob," he said. "I'm running in the Town Sports tomorrow, and I want to enter in the Two-Twenty Yards and the Quarter-Mile. They touch you half-a-crown a time as the entry fee."

"Bah, you hand it over, Alf Tupper!" shouted Aunt Meg. "I lets you keep half-a-crown, don't I?"

"I tell you, I want five bob!" retorted Alf.

"If you don't give it me, don't you come in this house again!" screeched Aunt Meg. "I kept you long enough before you earned any wages, didn't I? Come on, hand it over."

Alf pushed his hand into his pocket, took out two shillings and a sixpence, and threw them down on the table.

Alf shrugged.

"What's for supper?" he asked.

"I've got nothing in," said Aunt Meg. "You've money in your pocket, ain't you? Go and get your own supper."

Alf slouched out of the house into the shadows of Anchor Alley. The darkness was broken by the bright light shining through one of the windows. People were dotted around and there was the unmistakable smell of fish and chips.

Alf sniffed and moved towards the doorway of the fried fish and chips shop. Bert Bivens, a chap he knew, was in the shop, and asked Mrs Spicer for "sixpenn'orth of chips and a piece."

Alf did not miss a detail. Bert sprinkled salt and vinegar over his chips, then walked out of the shop, and stood on the pavement to eat his supper.

Alf's hand was in his pocket and his fingers shut round his half-crown.

Bert's jaws moved busily.

"Had your supper, Alf?" he asked.

Alf looked hungrily at the chips in Bert's piece of newspaper.

"Not yet," he said. "I don't know that I want any tonight."

"Ain't you hungry?" inquired Bert.

"Maybe a bit, but I'm in training," replied Alf. "It's the sports tomorrow."

"Come off it, a few chips won't spoil your wind," said Bert.

Alf opened his fingers. He let the half-crown slip back into his pocket. With a farewell nod to Bert, he shuffled off up the alley.

THE secretary of the Town Sports, sitting at a trestle table in the committee tent, was busy receiving the late entries.

Alf threw down his half-crown.

"Make it the Quarter-Mile, mister," he said.

"Name and club?" asked the secretary.

"Alf Tupper — and I don't belong to any club," replied Alf.

The secretary scooped the half-crown into the cash box and picked up his pen to attend to the next entrant.

The big crowd gathered in the small stadium had a thrill when the Granton Hall contingent arrived.

Commander Churcher was a firm believer that a smart display was good for morale. He himself led the twenty athletes who were to represent Granton Hall. Clem Gatacre carried the red and gold standard and was followed by the others, wearing their dark red blazers and white flannel trousers.

Alf sniffed as he watched.

"Swankers!" he growled. "What's the sense of all that dressing-up?"

The starters for the 100 Yards heats

were called. Howard Potter, who was in attendance, dashed off to the starting line and took charge of the track suits as the Granton Hall entrants peeled them off.

The running kit of the Granton men consisted of white singlets with badges and dark red borders, white shorts and dark red socks.

Somebody dropped a programme and Alf whipped it up. The information was not complete, but it did state that in the Quarter-Mile the Granton Hall representative would be Len Rayner, a former Public Schools Champion over the distance.

Alf's patched jacket was off in a second when the loudspeaker called up the starters in the Quarter-Mile.

Len Rayner, a dark, handsome fellow, zipped off his track suit and handed it to Howard. Vic Mason, who was running for the Harriers, stared coldly at Alf.

Alf was drawn beside Rayner and Mason.

At the gun, Rayner was away to a streamlined start. He snatched a narrow lead from Mason and held it in the early stages of the race.

Alf lost a bit of ground in getting away. He was third at the end of sixty yards.

The pace surprised Alf for it was the first time he had been in class company. He felt that he could hold it and followed Mason round. By halfway, the patter of feet behind him was fading.

The spectators started to shout as the three runners came round close enough for a tablecloth to have covered the lot of them, but with Rayner still comfortable in the lead.

Forty yards to go, Rayner quickened his stride into a spurt and went hard for the tape. Mason was out of it and dropped back. Alf took second place.

Commander Churcher, standing near the finishing line, stop-watch in hand, was calmly timing Rayner, when he saw a runner, whom he recognised as the trespasser, come up level with the leader and start to fight it out with him over the last ten yards.

Rayner flung himself at the tape, but Alf was up with him, and only spectators who were in a direct line with the tape were able to pick out the winner.

There was a hush as the judges' announcement was awaited. Alf, breathing fast, brushed back his tangled hair with his forearm.

The loudspeaker boomed.

"The placings in the Quarter-Mile were, First — Rayner; Second — Tupper; Third — Mason," roared the announcer.

Alf was turning away to pick up his jacket when he found Commander Churcher in front of him.

"What have you done to yourself, my lad?" demanded the Commander.

Alf looked down at the bloodstains slowly spreading across his left shoe.

"Aw, I spiked myself on the first bend," he muttered. "One of my spikes came right through my shoe."

The Commander glanced at his stop-watch, and then lifted his gaze to stare after Alf with a look of bewilderment on his face. This youngster had approached record time with an injured foot. What would he have done if he'd been perfectly fit?

JUST LIKE ALF TUPPER, THE 'TOUGH OF THE TRACK' STORIES RAN AND RAN, FIRST IN *ROVER* AND THEN IN *VICTOR*. BY THE EARLY 1960s, ALF'S ADVENTURES WERE IN PICTURES, BUT THERE WAS NO DOUBT THAT THE TOUGH WAS STILL ON THE RIGHT TRACK. IN FACT HIS POPULARITY WAS SO GREAT THAT HE KEPT RUNNING RIGHT INTO THE 1990s. THE STORY BELOW IS FROM MARCH 1963.

The mile started and Alf steadily cut down Evans' lead. Then on the last bend of the last lap, Evans cut loose and took the lead from a local lad called Wilson. Alf went after him . . .

Alf and Rakes-Tyler set the pace in the steeplechase. At the last water-jump, Rakes-Tyler was only a yard in the lead with Alf chasing him, when . . .

In this race Jones and Alf were in a class of their own and were soon out in front.

Suddenly . . .

# The Runners

In France — SO THIS IS FRANCE, EH? LOOKS MUCH THE SAME AS ANYPLACE ELSE. HOPE I AIN'T COME ALL THIS WAY FOR NOTHING, REG!

I HOPE SO TOO, ALF. I WOULDN'T MIND HAVING YOU IN THE TEAM INSTEAD OF A RESERVE.

With some small change in his pocket and a broad grin on his face, Alf boarded the plane for Aubigny.

The team were taken to the largest hotel in Aubigny. There, they sat down to a first-class meal — and Alf's table manners came in for some caustic comments from Phil Rakes-Tyler, a snobbish champion steeplechaser, who was a bitter enemy of the boy from the back streets.

SOME OF THE MANNERS AT THIS TABLE MAKE IT LOOK LIKE FEEDING TIME AT THE ZOO, CECIL.

MAYBE I AIN'T AS LAHDI-DAH AS YOU, RAKES-TYLER, BUT I'LL RUN YOU ANY DAY!

QUIET THERE! I'VE AN ANNOUNCEMENT TO MAKE. A WALK OVER THE CROSS-COUNTRY COURSE HAS BEEN ARRANGED FOR THIS AFTERNOON.

Later — THERE'S A BOTTLENECK! THE ONLY WAY TO RUN THIS RACE IS TO GET AMONG THE LEADERS EARLY.

MAYBE YOU'RE RIGHT, ALF, BUT I PREFER TO RUN AS A TEAM.

I DON'T KNOW WHY TUPPER KEEPS SHOUTING HIS MOUTH OFF. HE WON'T BE IN THE RACE. EVERYONE IN THE TEAM IS FULLY FIT.

JUST CARRY ON REG. ME LACE'S UNDONE. I'LL CATCH YOU UP.

SAY, BUD, HOPE I AIN'T BUTTING IN, BUT I COULDN'T HELP OVER-HEARING, AN' I RECKON YOU'VE GOT SOMETHING. THE RACE COULD BE WON OR LOST AT THAT BOTTLENECK.

YES, BUT JUST TRY TO TELL 'EM THAT! YOU'RE A YANK AIN'T YOU. WHAT TEAM ARE YOU RUNNING FOR?

I'M ON MY OWN. I'D HAVE BEEN RUNNING FOR CALLY UNIVERSITY, BUT WE COULDN'T RAISE A TEAM SO I'M A LONE WOLF SORT. WHAT THEY CALL AN INDEPENDENT ENTRANT.

ARE THEY STILL ACCEPTING ENTRIES?

SURE THING. I ONLY PUT MY ENTRY IN THIS MORNING. THE OFFICE IS AT THE HOTEL DE VILLE, THE TOWN HALL.

I'VE HAD ENOUGH OF THAT PLACE. I'M GOING FOR A STROLL.

The team looked over the course and returned to the hotel. But Alf was not comfortable in the posh hotel. He went out that evening and, at a small garage, he saw something that made his eyes gleam . . .

NO, NO, MATE. YOU'RE DOING IT ALL WRONG. HERE, LET ME HAVE A GO.

SEE, THAT'S HOW IT'S DONE.

GOOD! IT IS EASY WHEN YOU KNOW.

HEY, JULES!

CHEERIO THEN, POPPA. I ENJOYED MYSELF.

Poppa Hartman, the garage proprietor, was astonished to see Alf at work, but his son, Jules, explained. Poppa was delighted with the work Alf had done, and brought him more.

YOU WORK GOOD. YOU COME BACK, NO?

Next day, on a practice run . . .

THE TEAM TACTICS HAVE BEEN DECIDED. WE WILL STICK TOGETHER AND TRY TO FINISH AS A TEAM.

THAT'S CRAZY. YOU WANT TO LET BLOKES LIKE REG HERE RUN ALL OUT AND TRY TO FINISH HIGHER UP THE LIST. THE HIGHER HE FINISHES, THE MORE POINTS FOR THE TEAM.

THE TROUBLE WITH YOU, TUPPER, IS THAT YOU DON'T HAVE ANY IDEA OF TEAM RUNNING. THE IDEA IS TO HELP EACH OTHER ALONG RATHER THAN YOUR LONE-WOLF TYPE OF STUFF.

THE TROUBLE WITH YOU IS THAT YOU KEEP STICKING YOUR NOSE IN — AND YOU'RE LIABLE TO GET IT PUNCHED.

ENOUGH OF THAT, NOW! CONCENTRATE ON THE COURSE.

I CAN SEE WHAT HAMILTON MEANS. THIS IS THE MOST DIFFICULT COURSE I HAVE EVER SEEN.

The team finished their practice run round the course and returned to the hotel where they found a notice giving the full list of runners.

OH, I SEE VURMI, THE FLYING FINN, IS IN THE FINNISH TEAM. THEY'LL BE A FORMIDABLE LOT NOW.

TUPPER! YOU'VE PUT IN AN INDEPENDENT ENTRY.

AH, WHAT ABOUT IT? A BLOKE'S ENTITLED TO A RUN.

WE DIDN'T BRING YOU TO FRANCE, PAY YOUR FARE AND HOTEL BILL AND EVERYTHING, TO HAVE YOU RUN AGAINST YOUR OWN TEAM. WE'D BETTER GO AND SEE COMMANDER CHURCHER ABOUT THIS.

WELL, WHAT DO YOU EXPECT? YOU DON'T WANT ME STANDING WATCHING WITH MY HANDS IN ME POCKETS, DO YOU? THIS IS SUPPOSED TO BE A SPORT, AIN'T IT?

Commander Churcher was warden of Granton Hall and in charge of the team.

WE JUST CAN'T HAVE THIS, YOU KNOW, TUPPER. SUPPOSE YOU CAME IN NINETEENTH AND ONE OF OUR TEAM CAME IN TWENTIETH. YOU'D ROB THE TEAM OF A POINT.

AY, BUT I AIN'T IN THE TEAM SO I CAN'T BE AS GOOD AS THE BLOKES YOU PICKED. ON THAT REASONING, THEY'LL ALL FINISH IN FRONT OF ME, SO THE QUESTION WON'T ARISE!

I'M AFRAID, THOUGH I DO IT RELUCTANTLY, I MUST ASK YOU TO WITHDRAW YOUR ENTRY, AND LEAVE THE PARTY, TUPPER.

ASK AWAY, THEN. BUT IT WON'T DO YOU ANY GOOD. I'M HAVING A RUN! I CAN LOOK AFTER MYSELF. I DON'T NEED YOUR POSH HOTELS. YOU CAN KEEP 'EM!

SORRY THIS HAD TO HAPPEN, ALF.

GOOD RIDDANCE, I WOULD SAY.

YOU AIN'T RID OF ME, YET. AN' IF I DON'T BEAT YOU, I'LL GIVE UP RUNNING AND TAKE UP TIDDLEYWINKS.

THREE AND SIX — AN' ME RETURN TICKET. THAT'LL DO ME. I RECKON I KNOW WHERE I CAN MAKE A LIVING AN' I'LL STILL BEAT THAT RAKES-TYLER OR BURST!

ONLY A FEW MINUTES TO GO. BETTER TELL MILES HE IS RUNNING, FRANK.

NO, WAIT A MINUTE, SIR. THIS LOOKS LIKE TUPPER COMING NOW.

WILL YOU RUN FOR US, TUPPER? RAKES-TYLER HAS HURT HIS ANKLE AND HE HAS HAD TO WITHDRAW. WE NEED YOU FOR THE TEAM.

SO THE OLD SNOB'S COME A CROPPER, EH? WELL, I DON'T MIND TAKING HIS PLACE. I DON'T CARE WHO I RUN FOR.

WELL, WE WANT A TEAM VICTORY, TUPPER — AND THAT MEANS RUNNING AS A TEAM AND STICKING TOGETHER. TAKE YOUR PACE FROM REG FRY. NO ONE IS TO PASS HIM TILL NEAR THE END. THEN IT IS EVERY MAN FOR HIMSELF. GO ALL OUT AND TRY TO FINISH AS HIGH UP THE LIST AS POSSIBLE.

THAT BACKSTREET LOUT DOESN'T KNOW WHAT TEAMWORK IS. YOU MARK MY WORDS, HE'LL RUN FOR HIMSELF — AND BLOW THE TEAM!

HEY, WHAT'S GOING ON?

TIME TO LINE UP, LADS. THAT'S THE SIGNAL. THE MAN ON THE HORSE WILL DROP THE SHEAF AND THE CANNON WILL FIRE AGAIN AS A SIGNAL TO START. COME ON NOW. STICK TOGETHER.

HEY, ALF, YOU'RE GOING THE WRONG WAY. WE'RE DOWN HERE. THE TEAM HAS TO STICK TOGETHER, THAT'S THE FINNISH TEAM UP THERE!

I'VE JUST GONE A BIT DEAF, REG. THIS TEAM RUNNING WON'T WORK, NOT IF VURMI'S GOING TO CUT LOOSE. I'M GOING TO STICK WITH HIM.

They're off!

I THOUGHT YOU'D MAKE A BREAK FOR IT, MISTER VURMI, BUT YOU'RE NOT GOING TO GET EVERYTHING YOUR OWN WAY!

WELL I WON'T HAVE TO QUEUE TO GET THROUGH THE BOTTLENECK ANYWAY. HOPE REG FRY AND THE LADS ARE WELL PLACED.

I TOLD YOU THAT ROUGHNECK WAS NO USE TO THE TEAM. HE'S A LONE WOLF. ALWAYS HAS BEEN AND ALWAYS WILL BE. HE'LL RUN ONLY FOR HIMSELF — NEVER FOR A TEAM!

I'M AFRAID YOU MAY BE RIGHT. HE'S PAID NO ATTENTION TO THE TEAM TACTICS — AND AT THE RATE HE'S GOING, HE'LL SOON CRACK UP.

A few minutes later —

HERE THEY COME! TUPPER'S STILL LEADING — AND THEY'VE RUN AN AMAZINGLY FAST FIRST LAP!

VURMI IS BEING FORCED TO RUN FASTER THAN HE'D LIKE TO. MAYBE TUPPER KNOWS WHAT HE'S DOING AFTER ALL. BUT CAN HE KEEP IT UP FOR ANOTHER TWO LAPS?

YOU CAN NEVER TELL WITH TUPPER, SIR. BUT YOU CAN BE SURE OF ONE THING. HE'LL RUN TILL HE DROPS!

To everyone's amazement, Alf did maintain his cracking pace. Vurmi just could not get past him. Then, on the third lap, the strain began to tell.

AND WE ALL KNOW WHAT HAPPENS AT THE END OF PART ONE. RIGHT! IT'S TIME FOR THE ADVERTS, ONLY THESE ADS ORIGINALLY APPEARED IN **ROVER, WIZARD** AND **HOTSPUR** AROUND FIFTY YEARS AGO. SO DON'T HEAD DOWN TO YOUR LOCAL SHOP LOOKING FOR A VEST POCKET RADIO OR A SEEBACKROSCOPE, BECAUSE UNLESS TRADE'S BEEN VERY SLOW, THEY'LL HAVE BEEN SOLD OUT FOR DECADES.

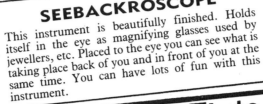
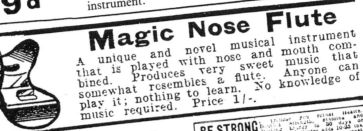

# THE TRUTH ABOUT WILSON

**A**T last I am able to tell the truth about Wilson. No more sensational figure ever appeared in sporting history. His name was on the lips of even those who ordinarily had not the least interest in athletics.

A few years ago this story would have earned me a fortune from the newspapers. Wilson was news. Everything that Wilson did, every fact that could be gleaned about Wilson was red-hot news.

Only now, with a world war intervening, have I ascertained the incredible truth about Wilson — only now can I reveal the astounding inside story of this man who smashed athletic records like cheap crockery and set standards which can never be equalled, let alone surpassed.

My first sight of Wilson, in common with eighty thousand other stupefied spectators, was at the British summer championship meeting held in London in the August of that year before the war when he burst into the limelight. At that time I was on the sporting staff of the "London Daily Clarion".

Old John Hawke, the sports editor, was the only other person in that paper-littered office about nine o'clock on the Saturday morning.

"You're covering the B.S.C. meeting at Stamford Bridge," he said gruffly.

"What's Arthur doing?" There was surprise in my voice. "He's never been known to miss —"

"Stone says he's exhausted of excuses for British defeats," replied the sports editor drily. "He says he's sick of writing columns to explain away the fact that Britain hasn't won the B.S.C. mile for years.

"As it is, I can use Arthur on another job, and your fresh brain can think of an apology for the British public."

I nodded a farewell to John and reached for my hat. I left the office wondering if I would see the American, Ron Gleebe, break his record — if only by a fifth of a second.

Little did I imagine just then that the afternoon would see speculation in fractions shattered, and that instead of half a column on the sports page I should be writing the main splash story for Page One. For in a few hours Wilson the unknown was going to blaze his name on the annals of sport.

Very soon, I was standing at the top of the steps which led down to the arena. Coming up the steps was a burly fellow about my own age. On his lapel was a badge bearing the word 'Steward'. The bridge of his nose was broken and it was my fist that had done the damage in an amateur boxing final three years before.

"Why hullo, Ducker!" I exclaimed.

"Hello, Webb," said Frank Ducker. "Would you like to watch the mile from the field?"

It was an invitation at which I jumped. It meant that instead of watching the mile from the press box high in the stand I should have a close-up view from the ground itself. My nod was eager.

"Then come on," he said.

We clattered down the steps and turned along the tunnel that led out into the open.

The white-coated starter examined the priming of his big starting pistol. The runners crouched at the take-off. There was a moment's pause. Then as the starter began to lift his arm I was aware of a slight commotion behind me. There was a shout of "Stop him!"

I turned round and was just in time to see a man drop over the barrier on to the track a short distance behind the runners. In that first glimpse I saw to my amazement that he seemed to be dressed for running. He had on a plain slack woollen singlet with half-length sleeves, and shorts which came to below the knee. He strode nearer, and I suddenly realised that his feet were bare.

The starter, gaze intent on the line-up, seemed to be unaware of the trespasser. His finger poised on the trigger. Bang! At the instant the runners got off the mark the stranger caught up to them and flashed over the starting line at Ron Gleebe's elbow.

I was not more than a dozen yards away, and I got my first full view of this amazing thirteenth runner in the race. He was little more than medium in stature, but the breadth of his chest impressed and I saw whipcord muscles standing out in his arms and legs. His neck was thin, which perhaps made his head seem large in proportion. His brown hair, sparse and without a parting, had a short fringe coming down straight over his forehead. From deep sockets stared eyes that were small and piercing. Over the prominent cheek bones the skin was stretched tight. In my ears, I can still hear that roar of amazement as eighty thousand people saw the field increased from twelve to thirteen.

"Don't spoil the race!" roared Ducker. "Grab him when he falls out!"

The stranger whom the world was soon to know as Wilson had gone ahead. His legs were a blur, his arms flashed like pistons as, with his head thrown back, he burst past Gleebe and took the inside of the track with a terrific sprint.

"He won't last long," snorted Ducker angrily. "He'll burn himself up!"

The unknown, however, showed no signs of flagging in the first hundred yards. At double that distance he was still going strongly. Every moment ought to have been his last in the race. I know I expected him to stagger aside and crumple up. So did everyone else with any knowledge of running. But as he entered the third hundred yards he was still drawing away from the field.

Gleebe was running second. Brown was his shadow, and Haki a yard further back. Behind them the others were beginning to straggle.

Round the curve ran Wilson to complete the first lap so far ahead of the rest that he seemed to be running the race on his own. I still expected to see him falter and fall out, but there was a rhythm about his running which told of the complete co-ordination of mind and body, and he flashed past us with the grace of a greyhound.

The loud-speakers boomed out. The announcer's voice was harsh with excitement.

"Times for lap one," he shouted. "The leader, the mystery runner, has covered the first quarter-mile in forty-five seconds —"

"It's impossible, fantastic!" he cried. "Forty-five seconds! Gosh — that beats the world record for the quarter-mile! It's wrong! Something's happened to the timing apparatus!"

Another steward turned, his face red with excitement.

"I thought something was wrong with my stop-watch, but it confirms that time," he gasped. "Look at him! Look at him! Still going like an express!"

The spectators were yelling like a cup final crowd. Some of you were there. Some of you shouted as loudly as the rest. You will remember how Wilson came round that circuit to finish the second lap in another forty-five seconds, with the famous Gleebe and the rest strung out yards and yards behind. But I was close to the track. I could have touched Wilson as he thudded by, and I stared for those traces of distress, the glazing eye, the trickle of saliva from panting lips that would have heralded the end. There was none. He was holding his sustained turn of speed without any signs of cracking up.

Wilson was the only man in the race. The others might not have been on the track for all the notice that was taken of them.

As Wilson went into the third lap two questions were on our lips — Would he last the mile? Who was he? However, at the moment, the first question overwhelmed the other. I know that as I watched him a cry of disappointment burst from me.

"He's slowing," I shouted.

"No!" Ducker yelled in my ear. "It's a trick of the light. He's in the shadow of the stand! Look! Look! He's as strong as ever!"

Ducker was right. Wilson finished the third lap, and the loudspeakers announced that he had again run the quarter-mile in forty-five seconds. The crowd was in a frenzy.

Three hundred yards to go, two hundred, one! I stepped forward to the side of the finishing tape. From that vantage point I could see Wilson clearly as he approached. His limbs were moving with unflagging impetus and, though I could see his chest heaving, he was still not gasping for breath. The crowd suddenly ceased to shout and watched tensely, on edge lest near the end something should rob the runner of his amazing triumph. In that strange hush I could hear the thudding of Wilson's bare feet on the track. The runner threw out his arms to breast the tape. Then the tape was fluttering from the hands of the judges. Wilson had won. Wilson had achieved his first shattering victory. The loudspeakers shrieked that the mile had been run in the incredible time of three minutes, and the crowd lifted up their voices in a shout that must have been heard halfway across London.

I saw Wilson stagger. As he lost his impetus he dropped on his knees. Then he swayed forward and lay prone on the track.

"Doctor! Doctor!" someone else was shouting, and two ambulance men with a stretcher came at the run.

I stooped and pulled him over. His eyes were shut. He seemed to be in some sort of coma. But even before the stretcher-bearers could arrive his eyelids lifted. He drew a sharp, deep breath and jumped to his feet.

"Did I —" he began.

"Yes, yes, you won," I cried.

Wilson's shoulders rose in a shrug as if the winning of the race did not matter.

"Did I run the mile in three minutes?" he demanded hoarsely.

"Yes," I said.

"Ah!" A long, drawn-out sigh of supreme satisfaction was uttered by Wilson. "Three minutes —" he muttered, as if to himself. "I have done what I set out to do!"

The officials had closed round him in a body. Above their babble I heard the announcement that Gleebe had knocked a fifth of a second off his own record, a feat that seemed laughable compared with Wilson's run.

Already the excited spectators were climbing over the fences and barricades to close in on Wilson, so we formed a group around him and forced a way towards the passage to the dressing-rooms.

Ducker slammed the door and turned the key.

"We can issue a statement later."

I grinned. It was a great stroke of luck that had put me on the inside of the story. John Hawke was going to get a pleasant surprise when the junior member of his staff produced the smashing narrative of the day's events. Wilson stood in the middle of the room. Someone handed him a glass of water, from which he just took a sip. My impression was that he was bewildered by all the fuss that was being made. Mr Sydney Tuke, the stout, florid chairman of the committee, spoke excitedly.

"We've got to decide if this man is the winner, gentlemen," he said. "We do not even know his name!" He turned to the runner. "What is your name?"

"Wilson," was the answer.

"Er, you are British?" exclaimed Tuke.

"Yes," was the monosyllabic reply.

"Who do you run for?" demanded Tuke.

Wilson looked puzzled.

"Who do I run for?" he echoed.

"I mean to say, don't you belong to a club?" asked Tuke.

Wilson shook his head.

"Then where do you come from?" demanded Tuke.

Wilson's answer was gruff.

"I want to go," he said. "Show me the way out!"

Tuke gasped.

"Doesn't it matter to you that you've just beaten the best milers in the world by an — er — incredible margin?" he demanded.

Wilson gave a disinterested shrug.

"It isn't the first three-minute mile," he stated.

"What?" gasped Tuke.

"In March of 1774 Benjamin Nutsford ran from the Gibbet Ash on Lambton Moor to Stayling Church in three minutes," continued Wilson definitely. "It was for a purse of fifty sovereigns subscribed by the gentry of Stayling."

Tuke gave a laugh.

"A village legend!" he declared. "There was no proper method of timing a race in those days."

"You will find his name in the parish register at Stayling if you care to look," he said. "And I know he ran the mile in three minutes, covering the last hundred yards while the church clock was striking three."

"I am going now," Wilson said. "Where are my clothes? I left them behind the fence."

"I'll get them," I volunteered.

I admit I did not make this offer merely out of kindness of heart. I was going to hang on to Wilson. He could give me the greatest athletics story of the era. Already, by a stroke of luck, I was on the inside of the story — the other reporters were all still literally outside, judging by the continued knockings on the door.

The arena was still in turmoil. The vast crowd still roared and swayed with excitement and the loudspeakers appealed in vain for order so that the next event, the 440 yards hurdles, could be started.

I got hold of a policeman, told him what I wanted, and we made our way along together outside the fencing. It was, however, an easy matter to find the spot. An excited Cockney, in a broken-brimmed cap, was telling his story to the people around him.

"It was just before the mile started that this guy shoved his way in front of me," the Cockney was saying. "Here, mate, who're you shoving, I asks. D'you mind taking your elbows out of my ribs, I says. He didn't say a word, no! He just dropped his clothes off an' was over the barrier quicker than I can sneeze —"

I cut into the story.

"Have you got his clothes?" I asked.

The Cockney glanced at the policeman.

"Here you are, mister," he said, and handed me a jacket and trousers which were made out of a thick, homespun yarn and a pair of clumsy thick-soled shoes.

"Is that all?" I inquired. "Hadn't he got a shirt — or socks?"

"No, that's the lot, guv'nor," declared the Cockney.

I thanked the officer for his assistance and hurried back to the dressing-room.

Wilson pulled on his clothes. Then he leaned towards me and whispered.

"Can you get me away from here?" he asked.

This was my opportunity, and I grabbed it.

"I've got my car in the car park," I answered softly. "Come along!"

I pressed a half-crown into the attendant's hand, and though he looked surprised, he let us out without the officials noticing. Along the maze of corridors I led the way.

I packed Wilson into my old sports car.

There was a lot of traffic about at the time, but nothing to worry an experienced driver, and I kept my foot down.

I glanced at Wilson. Instantly I slowed down. The man was plainly scared. He was sitting in a taut, strained attitude and with one hand was gripping the door handle.

"Sorry, old chap, I'll take it a bit easier," I said. "Actually I think you're safer in London than out in the country."

Wilson just nodded and relaxed a bit as I went even slower. An idea had formed in my mind. I turned into a side street and pulled up outside a Post Office.

"I shan't be a minute," I told him. "I want to make a phone call."

Fortunately there was a vacant telephone box inside the office, and in a matter of moments I was through to my sports editor.

"Look here, we want every scrap of information you can gather about this running wizard." Hawke burst out as soon as he heard my voice. "Do you think there's a chance of an interview?"

"Wilson's in my car now," I said.

"What?" Hawke's yell nearly split my eardrum. "You've got him to yourself? You've got an exclusive?"

"Listen, John," I went on. "Wilson's a queer sort of chap. He won't want a blaze of publicity, or to be accurate I doubt if he cares a bean. He's got to be handled carefully. I'm going to try and persuade him to come with me to the Gardner Gardens hotel — you know, that quiet little place off Russell Square. We ought to be able to talk there without interruption."

"Sure, sure. But what about photographs?" Hawke cut in. "We'll need all we can get —"

"Send one of the cameramen round to Gardner Gardens. Meantime I'll try and persuade Wilson to let the photographer take the pictures. We've got to be wary. He's a queer fish."

I hung up the receiver and hurried from the telephone-box. I was feeling on top of the world. I believed that I had gained Wilson's confidence and that he would talk to me about himself. I ran down the steps from the Post Office. Then I stopped dead.

I had a frozen feeling as I stared at my car. It was empty. Wildly my gaze turned up and down the street. Few people were about. Had Wilson been there I should have seen him immediately.

There was not a trace of anyone in homespun clothes and thick shoes. I felt numbed as I realised that Wilson had gone.

It was in a disgruntled and exasperated mood that I walked slowly to my car. I was opening the door when suddenly something caught my eye. A small object was lying on the floor by the side of the passenger's seat. I picked it up and found it was a notebook with a worn leather cover.

There was an inscription inside the cover. The ink had faded badly, and I had to turn it to the light to read:

"W. Wilfon, Amberfide Moor."

"Wilfon?" I muttered. "Amberfide — oh, I've got it! He must be an old-fashioned guy to write 'f' for 's'. Or maybe he didn't write it himself. Perhaps it belonged to his father or something."

Curiously I opened the notebook. The pages were closely covered with the same close writing, full of f's for s's, and difficult to read. But it did not make sense to me. I can still remember how the first page began —

"Witch-hazel (Hamamelif virginica) XIII and V; Atropa belladonna XV; Faxifraga (herba) XC and XII; Thymuf VII; Willow herb (Epilobium) XX; Digitalif, V. — "

The whole book was the same. It struck me as being the possession of an enthusiastic botanist who had listed all the herbs he had ever found. Still, I was not much concerned with the contents of the book. The great thing was that it gave me a clue to Wilson's possible whereabouts. He must have dropped his notebook as he made his hurried exit from my car.

Where was Amberside Moor? I had never even heard of it. I made a grab for my gazetteer and eagerly searched the "A's". "Ah! Got it!" I read:

"Amberside Moor, Yorkshire. This tract of wild and lonely country lies ten miles to the west of the Great North Road. The nearest Post Office is at Stayling (three miles), nearest station, Tuffton (nine miles)."

Yes, I was getting hot. I remembered abruptly that I had heard of Stayling for the first time earlier in the day. Wilson himself had mentioned it. It was to Stayling Church, he said, that Benjamin Nutsford had run in 1774.

I tossed the gazetteer into the car, dropped the notebook into my pocket, ran back to the telephone, and rang Hawke again.

"I've lost him, John," I admitted, then I continued before Hawke had a chance to bellow angrily down the phone. "Don't worry. I'm sure I can track Wilson down, and that's what I'm going to do, without a second's delay."

Hawke began to say something, but it was too late. I was already replacing the receiver.

I put up at Doncaster on my drive north, and it was about ten o'clock next morning that I approached Stayling along a narrow, winding lane.

I turned a corner and the lane widened out into the village street of Stayling.

Nobody seemed to be about.

Just then, a small boy with a dog at his heels came whistling towards me and stopped to look at the car.

"How fast does that go?" he asked, gazing at the long, streamlined bonnet.

"It has done a hundred on a racing track," I said.

"Gee, I'd like a ride in it," exclaimed the youngster.

"Well, perhaps I'll give you a lift when I find Mr Wilson," I said.

"I can tell you where he is," the boy declared eagerly. "I've just been up on the moors an' I saw him asleep by some bushes. You see the river there." He pointed towards the water flowing under a stone bridge at the end of the village street. "Keep by the river and you'll find him."

I set out eagerly. My strides soon carried me away from the village as I walked along the north bank of the river. The stream was wide, twenty feet or so, but for the most part shallow.

I found Wilson. About two miles from the village on the high bleak moorlands I saw him.

Yes, I had found Wilson, but he was still so near and yet so far. I was on the north bank; he was on the south, and between us was the river, at least twenty feet wide.

I was wondering what to do, when Wilson woke up. He opened his eyes, jerked up on to his elbow, and stared in my direction. With a bound he was on his feet.

Just for a moment I thought he was going to run away, but for that I was ready. I snatched the notebook out of my pocket and held it up for him to see.

"Found this in my car," I shouted.

The effect on Wilson was electric. He lifted his arms in an excited gesture. He stopped, picked up a large bundle in one hand, and began to run towards the river.

I had naturally expected to see him wade across. Suddenly I realised that he had another intention, as his pace increased, his stride lengthened. He bent a trifle at the knees. A gasp broke from me as I watched his take-off from the further bank. I jumped back to give him a place to land, and he completed the jump by coming down lightly and regaining his balance with a little skip.

"I thank you for bringing me my notebook," he said. "I did not miss it until I had left London — it is very valuable to me."

"I'm glad you did lose it," I replied. "It enabled me to find you. Why — er — did you slip away from me?"

"I wanted to start my journey back home," stated Wilson. "I had a long walk in front of me."

"You've — you've come from London since yesterday afternoon?" I cried. "Why, it's the best part of two hundred miles! How long have you been back here?"

"Only an hour or two," Wilson answered. "That's why you found me sleeping. I'm usually up at sunrise."

I really did not know whether to believe Wilson or not. At the most he could not have been more than fifteen hours on the journey.

Wilson was looking at me. His eyes, deep in their sockets, had a piercing quality. There was something undefinable about the man. His attitude was so detached and calm. He had a poise and culture that a mere vagabond would not have possessed.

"Why have you come here?" he asked. "Was it only to give me back my notebook?"

"No." I said bluntly. "I am a newspaper reporter. All the world wants to read about you. Everyone wants to see your photograph. Wilson, you're famous —"

His shrug cut me short.

"I am in your debt for the return of my book," he said. "Write what you please. It is apparently what you want to do, but you will not say where I have my home."

"No fear," I blurted out. "That will be my secret." I paused a moment. "Would you let me take your photograph?"

"All right," he consented.

I did not give Wilson the chance to reconsider his decision.

I was delighted at the chance of securing this scoop.

"Is it true that you live out here in the open, summer and winter?" I asked as I slipped the camera away.

Wilson gave a nod.

"And that you live off nuts and berries?"

"There are other things to be found in the country besides nuts and berries," he said.

"Have you got any future plans?" I demanded. "Are you going to run again?"

"Will you be of help to me?" he asked. "Will you let me know when the big athletic contests are taking place — the really big ones. I have some difficulty in discovering when and where they take place."

"Of course," I said, eager to maintain a contact with Wilson. "But how shall I let you know?"

"Write to me at Stayling Post Office," he replied. "I will collect the letters myself."

"This means that you do intend to run again?" I said.

"I may. I may not," he said vaguely.

Then abruptly he seemed to remember something. He leaned down and unfastened his bundle. He fumbled inside and then brought out a worn leather case in shape rather like a satchel.

"Did you think I was telling a fairy tale when I spoke about Benjamin Nutsford?" he asked.

"Well —" I spluttered weakly.

"Here is the proof," he said, and took a sheet of yellowish, crinkled paper from the satchel.

I took it, and with difficulty read the faded writing.

The Eleventh of March, 1774.

"We who fign here hereby folemnly affirm that we have thif day been witneffef to the feat of Benjamin Nutfford, who ran from the Gibbet Afh to the Parifh Church of Stayling in three minutef dead, and accomplifhed the laft hundred yardf while the clock ftruck three.

Jaf. Yardley, rector.
A. Falby, Squire of Stayling
Wm.Wilfon, clerk to the Manor.

"Gosh, this is mighty interesting," I said. "I would like to publish it, but it would give away the fact that you're connected with Stayling. I suppose your family has been here for years?"

Wilson gave a nod. He held out his hand for the paper.

"I showed it to you to prove I wasn't telling a fairy story," he said. "Now, I'm going." He picked up his bundle which seemed to contain all his possessions. "Good-bye."

"Good-bye, and many thanks," I exclaimed, as with a long, fast stride, Wilson walked away across the moors. I stood and watched until he reached the top of a slope. Quickly he sank on the other side from view, and I was left wondering when I should see him again.

**THE MYSTERIOUS ATHLETE WAS TO RE-APPEAR MANY TIMES OVER THE YEARS. ONE OF THE MOST MEMORABLE OCCASIONS WAS IN 1965 AS A PICTURE STORY IN THE PAGES OF *HORNET*.**

IT IS GRAND TO BE HOME. THE CITIES ARE NOT FOR ME. EVEN THE AIR PEOPLE BREATHE THERE HELPS TO KILL THEM.

I HAVE BEEN LOOKING FORWARD TO THIS.

Later—

THESE HERBS WILL MAKE THE BROTH TASTY AND HELP ME TO REGAIN MY STRENGTH.

The mystery man of the moors ate his broth of herbs and natural foods. This was followed by some freshly-plucked berries. He then fell into a deep, refreshing sleep.

Next day Wilson leapt the twenty-foot-wide stream near his cave.

SHORT OF MY MARK. I NEED MORE LONG JUMP PRACTICE. BUT FIRST I MUST TEST MY STAMINA.

For hours, the man named Wilson raced across the moors, then he came to a high wall.

RODDIE FERGUSON'S LEAP. PERHAPS WITH THE SPUR OF COMPETITION — YES, NOW WHAT IS THE NAME OF THAT MAN? FRANK DUCKER — THAT'S HIS NAME. PERHAPS I WILL COMMUNICATE WITH HIM . . .

FERGUSON'S LEAP
THIS PLAQUE COMMEMORATES THE FINE FEAT OF RODERICK FERGUSON, DALESMAN, WHO JUMPED A HEIGHT OF 7 FEET 6 INCHES TO CLEAR THIS WALL. ERECTED BY AMAZED AND ADMIRING FRIENDS WHO WITNESSED THE FEAT.
W. WILSON, CLERK OF THE PARISH OF STAYLING.

Two days later the committee of the Amateur Athletics Association were gloomily discussing Britain's prospects in the International Meeting at Belle Vue, Manchester, the following Saturday, when Frank Ducker burst in.

ITALY IS A CERTAINTY FOR THE HIGH JUMP. FRANCE WILL TAKE THE 5000 METRES AND — WHAT ARE YOU DOING, DUCKER?

YOU CAN CHALK UP A WIN FOR BRITAIN IN THE 1500 METRES. LOOK WHAT'S ON THIS POSTCARD I'VE JUST RECEIVED!

*I shall be at Belle Vue on Saturday.*
*W. Wilson.*

Britain's most bizarre athlete continued his training miles from the nearest house, on the Yorkshire Moors.

IT IS TIME I RETURNED TO WHAT PEOPLE CALL CIVILISATION. I NEED COMPETITION. PERHAPS IT WILL PROVIDE THE SPUR I SEEK.

PURE, REFRESHING WATER AND WHOLESOME, NATURAL FOOD! THAT IS THE LAST I WILL HAVE TILL I RETURN!

All through the night, Wilson headed towards Manchester. Alternately running and walking, he ate up the miles at a fantastic rate.

Next day, at Belle Vue . . .

WHERE IS WILSON THEN, DUCKER? WHEN IS HE GOING TO TURN UP? HE'S MISSED THE PARADE ALREADY.

U.S.A

HE'LL TURN UP IN TIME TO WIN THE 1500 METRES, WEBB. DON'T WORRY. REMEMBER, HE APPEARED FROM THE CROWD LAST TIME.

IT'S NO USE. WE CAN'T WAIT ANY LONGER. WILSON HAS LET BRITAIN DOWN. WE'LL HAVE TO NOMINATE JACK HERBERT AS BRITAIN'S REPRESENTATIVE IN THE 1500 METRES.

Britain got off to an unexpected win in the 100 metres. The United States won the quarter mile. In international contests, points are only given for a win, so that the score was one point each to Britain and the United States when the time came for the 1500 metres. This was the key event of the afternoon — and still there was no sign of Wilson!

# WILSON

A WONDERFUL JUMP! MAZO HAS EQUALLED HIS OWN WORLD RECORD. NOW, WHAT CAN WILSON DO AGAINST THAT?

WHAT'S WILSON DOING NOW? HE'S INTERFERING WITH THE BAR.

Steadily the bar rose higher until it reached 6 feet 10 inches. By then only Toni Mazo and Wilson were left. The Italian had to equal his own record if he were to defeat this strange Britisher.

WHAT ARE YOU PLAYING AT, MAN? YOU HAVE PUT THE BAR TO 7 FEET 7 INCHES. THAT IS THE HEIGHT YOU WILL BE REQUIRED TO JUMP.

THAT IS THE HEIGHT WHICH I WISH TO ATTEMPT.

HE MUST BE MAD. HE'S RAISED THAT BAR TO AN IMPOSSIBLE HEIGHT.

HE IS TAKING A LONG RUN THIS TIME. THIS WILL BE HIS GREAT EFFORT.

HE'S DONE IT! WHAT A JUMP!

AT LAST, RODDIE. AT LAST!

HE HAS COLLAPSED — JUST AS HE DID AT STAMFORD BRIDGE AFTER HIS MILE!

DID I —?

YES, YOU MADE IT — A MAGNIFICENT LEAP! MAGNIFICENT INDEED!

NOW WHAT DID HE MEAN BY "AT LAST, RODDIE. AT LAST!" HE'S A PUZZLE, THAT ONE. BUT WHAT AN ATHLETE! WHAT A WORLD-BEATER BRITAIN HAS IN WILSON!

Wilson was overwhelmed with congratulations and invitations to functions, but refused them all. All he wanted to do was return to his native moors without any fuss. Frank Ducker smuggled him out of a side entrance so that he could escape the attention of his eager fans.

# The Runners

# BRUCE TULLOH

Wilson's barefoot running inspired real-life athlete Bruce Tulloh when he read *WIZARD* as a boy. Bruce's own story was told in the pages of *VICTOR* and The Observer newspaper.

BARE-FOOTED RUNNER, BRUCE TULLOH, WAS ONE OF BRITAIN'S HOPES IN THE MIDDLE-DISTANCE RANGE. HE WAS BORN IN DATCHET, BUCKINGHAMSHIRE.

## TULLOH'S GREAT SLOG ACROSS THE STATES

BRUCE TULLOH former 5,000-metres European champion, used to be known as the man who ran in bare feet. Then in 1960 he put some shoes on and ran across America.

It took him only 65 days to cover 2,900 miles from Los Angeles to New York. Then he came home and wrote a book about it.

One of the people who inspired this marathon never existed, but he set a very hot pace. Tulloh describes him as the great Wilson, a fictional athlete . . . of the boy's comic 'Wizard'. Wilson was not only 'a slim ageless figure', but he jumped higher, longer, and ran faster than anyone on earth. Tulloh points out that Wilson's magical feats (the period is the thirties) "have been improved upon in real life."

But it was Wilson's feats of endurance that did the touch that crowned the fantasy. After beating the best in the world in London Wilson did a modest 200-mile jog back to his native Yorkshire in his tweeds and heavy shoes. How very fitting. As Tulloh says "many of his greatest achievements were done purely for his own satisfaction."

At 13, Bruce started competitive running with a mile race at a village fete.

GRAND FETE

POOR KID, HE DOESN'T STAND A CHANCE

HE'LL DROP OUT HALF-WAY

TEAS

But Bruce did finish. Not only that, he beat most of his older rivals, to come in fourth!

Going on to specialise in the three-mile race, Bruce started running barefooted again — on cinder as well as grass tracks. In 1958 and 1959, he was first in the English Universities three-mile event. He broke the British record, and he went on to shatter the European, U.K. all-comers, U.K. national and A.A.A. national records with a time of 13 minutes, 12 seconds.

# THE BIG 5

That was the affectionate nickname given to *ROVER, WIZARD, ADVENTURE, HOTSPUR* and *SKIPPER* during the 1930s. It was even more appropriate at Christmas when all five produced chunky annuals packed cover to cover with action and fun.

Well, Jimmy, these are the Best Books of the Year. Which will You Have?

Blowed if I know, Dad— They're all so jolly good. CAN'T I HAVE THE LOT?

Adventure fans didn't always have to wait until Christmas to buy a book featuring their heroes. In the early 1960s, some of the most popular stories found their way into a series of paperbacks known as RED LION LIBRARY.

# DAYS

COMPARE THESE TWO PLAYGROUND SCENES ... THE PUPILS OF RED CIRCLE SCHOOL, SMARTLY DRESSED AND POLITE, IN *HOTSPUR* OF 1946 ... AND THE KIDS FROM KINGSWAY COMPREHENSIVE, SCRUFFY, WILD AND GIVING THEIR TEACHER A HARD TIME IN *CHAMP* FORTY YEARS LATER.

NOT MUCH IN COMMON AT A GLANCE, BUT ONCE YOU'VE READ THESE TWO TALES OF SCHOOLDAYS, YOU'LL DISCOVER THAT WHATEVER THE DECADE, BOYS WILL BE BOYS!

Red Circle School

A WISE guy once remarked that some people are born to trouble. He must have been thinking of people like me when he said it.

It's my misfortune that what I don't know about getting into trouble could be written on the price-tab of a tom-tit's bathing costume, and leave quite a sizeable margin. My father is never tired lecturing me about it, and says there are times when he feels I'll be the death of him. And there are other times when he feels like being the death of me.

He pretends to be reasonable about it, of course, and says he wouldn't mind my being the world's dumbest dunce so much, if only I wouldn't keep on getting into scrapes. But it's not my fault that trouble's my middle name, and I'm writing this story to prove it. And when I tell you of all the bother I landed in from the first moment of my arrival at Red Circle School, and leave you to judge whether I was to blame or not, I'll wager a flotilla of whales to a brace of tiddlywinks you'll give me the verdict.

Red Circle was to be my last chance when we came home from the East, and Dad threatened all sorts of dire penalties if I didn't make good there.

Well, I got off on the wrong foot right from the start on the day I went to Red Circle. On the train going down, for instance, I ran foul of a nasty type of gent who plainly had never been a boy himself. He was plumpish and wore a black moustache and a scowl which he handed to me when I sat down opposite him. We were alone in the carriage, and he nearly bit my nose off when I started whistling as the train moved out, and told me boys should be seen and not heard.

Then he began dozing, and I sat gazing at a pimple as big as a bean on his nose. The more I looked at that pimple, the more the blessed thing fascinated me, and I couldn't take my eyes off it. I had a pea-shooter in my pocket, and for five minutes I battled nobly with temptation. But it was no use, I simply couldn't resist it. I got out the pea-shooter, took careful aim, and let fly.

Whizz! Smack!

"Wow!"

He nearly hit the roof of the carriage with the leap he gave. It was no use trying to look innocent, hoping he'd think a wasp or something had stung him. I had shoved the pea-shooter back in my pocket too hurriedly, and one end of it was sticking out to give me away. Luckily, I'm pretty quick off the mark, and I was out of that carriage and down the corridor like a mosquito in a hurry when he made a furious dive at me.

Naturally I didn't expect ever to see him again when I got off the train at Lington, the station for Red Circle. So, when I saw Pimple-Nose on the platform, too, I thought it wiser to hang back until he had buzzed off.

He did so, in the only taxi available. I took a poor view of this as I felt that it was only right that I should arrive at my new school in some sort of style.

At that point I spotted one of those rough-riding Yankee war buggies — a jeep. The G.I. sitting at the wheel had a kind look so I oozed over and asked if he would be passing Red Circle School and if so, would he give me a lift. My luck was in. The Yank was a nice type. He just had to collect some stuff from the station and then we were on our way.

I'm a chap who likes to try everything once, so I was soon angling for a chance to drive the jeep. You may have gathered that I can hand out the honey-talk when required, and you will remember I remarked that the G.I. was a good guy. Anyway, the result was that soon I was sitting behind the wheel.

This was grand. I concluded I was the only Red Circle chap to arrive driving a jeep.

We soon reached the school which is just about two miles from Lington. I thought I had the knack of driving a jeep now so, to create an impression, I stood up on the seat and drove through the gates with one foot on the wheel.

Lads who had been standing at the gates scattered like lightning and, with a chuckle, I got down and put on the brake.

At least that's what I thought, but actually I stood on the accelerator. The jeep shot into the quad as if it were jet-propelled. There were quite a lot of chaps standing about. They didn't stand long. They had to dive for their lives out of the way, and in two seconds that peaceful quad was a scene of pandemonium.

I hate to admit it, but definitely the jeep was out control. It was heading straight for the steps leading into what I discovered was Home House, and I could do nothing to stop it.

Of course I waved cheerfully to all the chaps just to reassure them and to save my face, but I was only putting on an act. I thought we would stop at the steps. But

no! These jeeps certainly are hot. This one was red-hot. It bumped up the steps with no bother at all.

I may say that all this time the Yank had been trying to get back into his seat, having been tossed into the back by the sudden jerk.

We were halfway up the steps when a master appeared in the doorway. There was something familiar about him but he didn't stop to be identified. He turned and ran. He was quite right to do so for the jeep reached the top of the steps and careered into the building. I saw we were in a hall, but what fascinated me was the master in front. I had recognised him. He was Pimple-Nose.

I don't quite know how the affair would have ended if the Yank hadn't managed to clamber back to the front seat. Perhaps Pimple-Nose would have kept ahead of the jeep until it ran out of gas. Perhaps it would have crashed. Anyhow the Yank soon stopped it. He seemed to be taking a dim view of the whole business but I had no time to devote to him. Pimple-Nose had grabbed me and had introduced himself in thunderous tones as Mr Smugg, the master of Home House, the very house I was going into.

You should have seen his expression when he discovered that Edward Jones, his new pupil, was the cheeky young scamp who had blitzed a jeep round his own hall! It was quite a while before he got his breath back, and told me to come along to his study.

The term was a fortnight old. The house master had been away on business, and was returning when I met him on the train, without knowing who he was. I had made a very bad start, and all I could do was try to mend matters with an apology.

"I'm frightfully sorry, sir," I said, meekly, as soon as I could get a word in. "I didn't know who you were, and anyway, I wasn't really aiming at your pimple. I was aiming at a fly over your head, and you happened to move it at the wrong moment — your head, I mean, not the fly. And as for the jeep, sir, it ran away, and how was I to know how much the war has done to advance mechanical science. Don't you think so, sir?"

"That will do," he rasped, breathing hard. "Your explanation is unconvincing, and your apology does not deceive me. You can thank your stars it is your first day here, or you would get a flogging. As it is, I will consider letting you off with a gating."

He then announced he was going to ask me some general test questions, to find out how good — or bad — a scholar I was.

I hadn't liked old Smugg from the start, but when I heard this I liked him even less.

Of course, it would have been all right if I had answered the questions to his satisfaction, but as usual I made a mess of it. It seems I was wrong in thinking Sir Walter Raleigh was a bicycle manufacturer, for instance, though I still maintain he had no business going about with a monicker like that if he wasn't. I was wide off the mark, too, in crediting Christopher Columbus with the discovery of Australia, and I've never thought the same of Columbus since for letting me down.

I fell down similarly on other

questions, and I could see Smuggy getting madder and madder with every question. Then he tried me with a mental arithmetic test, asking me if a herring and a half cost three-ha'pence, how much would a dozen cost?

This mental arithmetic stuff always makes my head reel, and in any case you can't buy half a herring anywhere. I thought it only right and reasonable to point this out to him, but it only seemed to make the old bounder madder than ever, and he threatened to pitch into me with a cane if I didn't answer the question.

Well, I did my best to solve the problem, but after chewing on it for a bit, I forgot the way he had put it, and asked him whether it was herrings he had said, or mackerel. He pretty nearly blew up at that, and the atmosphere was fairly sizzling for the next five minutes, while he told me what he thought of me, and I wasn't half relieved when he dismissed me at last, remarking grimly that he could see there was going to be trouble with me.

He wasn't the only one who could see there was going to be trouble. Personally, I could not only see it, but feel it and smell it. But, bless you, if I worried about things like that, I'd be pushing up daisies by now, because trouble's always on the horizon as far as I'm concerned.

A few minutes later I was in the Fourth Form quarters. I had forgotten to find out where I was to dig, so I moseyed up and down outside the studies for a while, to meet some of my new schoolfellows, who would put me wise.

But I didn't meet a soul, and everything seemed dead quiet. This surprised me, for I had heard some lively yarns about the doings of the Home House fellows.

I always get impatient when nothing is happening, so I grabbed the door handle of Study Two, and flung open the door. There were three lads inside, and they looked up in anything but a friendly fashion as I barged in.

"Is this a morgue I've dropped into, or a public school?" I inquired. "Is anybody alive in the joint?"

They didn't like this, and their frowns showed it.

"So you're the new chap," said one of them. "The one the kids have christened Jeep. Bit fresh for a newcomer, aren't you?"

This was a new one on me but there was nothing I could do about it.

"What do you expect me to do, creep round on my hands and knees till someone condescends to take notice of me?" I demanded.

"Well, you'd better not keep on bursting into other fellows' studies like that without so much as by-your-leave, or you'll find yourself in a morgue quick enough!" snapped another. "Only you won't know it."

If I have one fault, it is that I'm quick-tempered, and that made me flare up. But I calmed down again almost as soon. After all, it was my first day at Red Circle, and I didn't want to start by pushing anyone's face in.

"Keep your wool on," I said. "All I want is someone to tell me which study I'm supposed to go to."

"Well, that's simple," said the lad who had first spoken. "All the studies have two or three occupants at the moment, with the exception of Study One. There's only one fellow there, a chap named Macgregor, and no doubt he'll be glad to have you."

"Then Study One's the place for me. Thanks a lot. I'll be seeing you. Chin-chin!" I said, and tootled off.

I suppose they thought they were fooling me, but they weren't, not quite. I had seen the wink that passed from one to the other, and the grin that answered the wink, so I could see there was some joke about sending me to Study One. Maybe this Mick Gregor was a tough egg, who they expected would take the starch out of me, or something like that. Well, I'd soon find out.

A couple of ticks later I blew into Study One, where I found a tall, well-made fellow sitting at the table, writing. I may as well say at once there was a clean, hard look about this lad that I liked at once. But I didn't at all like the cold way he eyed me as I breezed in.

"So you're Mick Gregor," I said affably. "Pleased to meet you, old sport."

He gave me a look that nearly bored a hole in me.

"Macgregor is the name," he retorted icily, "Rob Roy Macgregor, of the Clan Gregor, and I'll thank you to remember it."

"OK, Macgregor it is," I said. "Some funny handles around here, I must say. Mine's Jones, by the way — and I understand they've tacked 'Jeep' on to it. I don't mind. Rough going suits me best," I added.

"That's lucky for you, because you'll certainly find the going very rough here if you don't lose some of your freshness pretty quick. We don't like newcomers to be too cocky here. Now scram!"

"Scram nothing. I'm staying here," I informed him. "I'm told you're on your lonesome, so I'm going to be your study-mate."

His eyes grew more like icicles than ever.

"I hear you've been out East, or something, so I'll make allowances," he said frigidly. "You don't understand. No one shares this study with me. I'm the Captain."

"Captain, general, or private, it's all the same to me," I assured him. "Bless you, I'm not particular. So thaw yourself at the fire, old horse, and start getting a bit sociable."

Macgregor jumped up, and if his eyes had been glinting before, there were sparks flying from them now.

"Listen, Jones," he said. "I don't like your face, I don't like your voice, and above all, I don't like your freshness. Now get out, or I'll throw you out!"

Well, my temper isn't built to stand that sort of talk from anyone, and it got me on the raw.

"Oh, yeah?" I snorted. "Go ahead and let's see you do it."

He didn't think twice about accepting the invitation, and before I knew what was happening, I was sprawling on my back in the passage, put there by a half-shove, half-punch that knocked me kicking. And the three bright sparks who had directed me to Study One were there to see me bite the dust, grinning all over their dials.

That tore it. It's always been my claim that I never look for trouble. But I lap it up when it comes my way. And anything in the nature of a scrap is right up my street.

I'm not boasting, but I've got a kick in my foot that'd surprise you, and a right hook that would give an ox the head-staggers. But I've often taken heavy punishment at the start of a fight by letting my temper get the better of me, and I made that mistake now.

I scrambled up fighting mad, and went for Macgregor like a whirlwind, only to be stopped in my tracks by a straight left between the eyes that made me see stars. Through the stars I saw him measuring me for a right to the jaw, and blocked it quickly with my hunched shoulder. But his left followed again like a steam-hammer and the floor jumped up and hit me.

"Sorry to have to do this, Jones," said Macgregor, standing over me. "I hope it'll teach you a lesson."

Teach my grandmother. It was himself who was going to get the lesson, though he didn't realise it yet. He didn't know me, or he wouldn't have thought me licked so easily.

He saw his mistake next moment, and there was surprise in his eyes, and maybe a touch of something like respect, when I got up for more.

His left whistled over my head as I ducked it. Then, in a flash, I was under his guard, and rocked him with a smack on the chin that sent him teetering back on his heels, in beautiful position for a sleeping-draught, which I lost no time sending over.

I'll hand it to him — he was fast, and tough as shoe leather. He dodged the passport to dreamland by a miracle of recovery and speed, and his left stabbed again to my face. And then, just as we were warming up, there was the swish of a gown in the passage, on the fringe of the crowd that had gathered, and old Smugg's voice broke up the party.

I needn't tell you how the old bird ranted and raved at me for fighting on my first day at school. The upshot was that Macgregor and I were awarded five hundred lines each, and everyone else in the passage got a hundred.

But I needed no telling the affair wasn't going to end there. Macgregor seemed to be the big noise in Home House, and I could see I had gone up in his estimation through the way I had stood up to him. The others were rather impressed, too. But I could also see with half an eye that in spite of this they were all shirty with me, thought me too cocky by a mile, and they were all incensed over their lines, Macgregor especially. So I wasn't surprised when a chap sitting next to me at supper (it had been rather late when I arrived) tipped me off that I was booked for a hot time in the immediate future.

"I wouldn't be in your socks for a million," he said, with a grin. "Macgregor will probably invite you into the gym tomorrow to finish that scrap, and he'll lam the daylights out of you. Meanwhile, look out for squalls in the dorm at bedtime. Home House doesn't like your cockiness, the fellows are annoyed over their lines and you're going to be smacked down tonight."

I had taken a genuine liking to Macgregor. It would be a pleasure to fight him any old time, but I always enjoy a scrap with a real fighter. But let tomorrow take care of itself. The hint about what was afoot in the dorm tonight was what concerned me most at the moment.

I had found my bed and locker earlier, and left my things there. I was last up when bedtime came. The dormitory door was a little ajar. They were all inside, but everything was quiet. They were waiting for me.

I stood for a while, wondering what was cooking inside. Then there was a footfall behind me, and I turned round. I'm blessed if it wasn't Smuggy again. That man seemed to be everywhere.

"What are you standing there for, Jones?" he rasped unpleasantly. "That is your dormitory. I will go in with you, and show you your bed, if you haven't already found it."

Some lucky instinct kept me from telling him I didn't need his services, and I stood aside.

"After you, sir," I said politely.

He pushed open the door. Instantly there was a bang, clatter, and swoosh, and he was deluged in a choice assortment of ink, soot, water, and suds, tipped on to his head from a basin balanced on the door.

Boy, oh boy, was I glad I had been so polite! Smuggy had walked into a booby-trap intended for little me, and as far as I was concerned he was welcome to it.

Gosh, you never saw such a commotion in your life. Smuggy nearly went wild. A frothing tiger would have been tame by comparison. I couldn't for the life of me keep in my mirth at the sight he presented, and for a second I thought he was going to brain me with the basin for laughing at him. As for the Fourth, the abuse he hurled at them nearly turned the air blue, and what he threatened to do to them in the morning lacked nothing except boiling in oil, as he tore off to the nearest bathroom to clean himself.

I was still laughing as I crossed to my bed, but the others weren't, and I didn't altogether blame them. The glares they bestowed on me would have sunk the "Queen Mary".

"Funny, isn't it?" snarled Ginger Robertson.

"Funny is the word," I chuckled. "But I must be the only guy here with a sense of humour. You fellows aren't exactly splitting your sides."

Macgregor came forward, his face like a thundercloud.

"It seems you're destined to be Public Headache Number One at Red Circle, Jones," he snapped. "You've landed the whole bunch of us in the soup now. There'll be red ructions over this in the morning with Smuggy."

"So sorry," I said. "Next time you arrange a booby-trap for me, let me know about it beforehand, and I'll make sure nobody else gets the benefit of it."

"Keep your sorrow for yourself," barked West. "You'll need it in about two jiffies. You've escaped the booby-trap, but by Jupiter, you won't escape the ragging you're going to get now!"

I suppose from their point of view I had asked for it, by being too cocky since I hit Red Circle. So their attitude wasn't surprising. But Jeep Jones doesn't show the white feather to anyone and I was on the point of telling them to go ahead and be blowed to them, when my eyes became riveted on a small box with air-holes which I had left on my locker earlier.

The box was on the floor now, open and empty. But it hadn't been empty when I left it on the locker.

"Suffering snakes!" I ejaculated, aghast. "Who threw that box off my locker?"

"Someone knocked against your locker, probably. What does it matter, anyay — what's the excitement about? The darn thing's empty."

"But it wasn't empty when I left it there!" I cried, in wild alarm. "I brought a tarantula all the way home from the East in that box, and now it's escaped!"

The Homers jumped as if stung, electrified.

"A wha-a-at?" croaked Robertson, when he found his voice.

"A tarantula. And a tarantula's the deadliest insect on earth. A single bite makes a job for an undertaker. My sainted aunt, where has it got to?" I said, searching feverishly all round my bed and locker.

"Great pip! Mean to say you had the nerve to bring a deadly insect like a tarantula here, and into the dorm, confound you!" howled Tony West.

"Don't ask fool questions. It was safe enough in the box. How was I to know some clumsy interfering fathead was going to knock it over? My hat, this is awful!" I got down on my knees to look under the bed. "The lock must have sprung when the box hit the floor, or else it was defective, and needed seeing to."

"I should jolly well think it must have needed seeing to, and so does your brain," hooted Ginger Robertson.

"Oh, shut up! Gimme a hand to look for it, quick, for goodness sake, everyone, and don't stand there like a squad of paralysed penguins!"

My word, I don't think there was ever such a scene in that dorm as the one that followed. The Fourth would have scalped me if it hadn't been for the urgent necessity of recapturing the tarantula before it did harm, and they swore they'd settle my hash immediately the tarantula was accounted for. But then, they had been going to settle my hash already, so I lost nothing on that score.

As for the search itself, you never saw anything like it. Every bed in the dorm

was gone over inch by inch, gingerly but thoroughly, every hole and corner examined, every nook and cranny peered into. The only thing we didn't do, in fact, was take up the floorboards.

But the search was utterly fruitless, and after an hour's feverish hunt, the tarantula was still at large. None of the Fourth could think of sleep with such a deadly creature in their midst; the very name of the tarantula, the killer spider, made their flesh creep; and I was nearly being pulverised when I wanted them to leave it till the morrow and go to bed, on the off-chance that the tarantula might return quietly to the box of its own accord when peace was restored.

Finally, someone went and blew the gaff to Mr Smugg. And that, of course, fairly put the tin hat on it. Smuggy was by this time looking on me with anything but loving tenderness, and if anything was needed to convince him I was bad news, it was this. Sniping on his pimple in the train, chasing him with a jeep, scrapping with Macgregor on my first day, the booby-trap he had walked into through me, the proof I had given that I was going to be the worst dunce he had ever handled — all this hadn't exactly endeared me to him, and the tarantula was the last straw.

He didn't endanger his skin by coming to the dorm himself, but sent for me; and the tongue-lashing he gave me when I went nearly blistered me. He called me every name he could think of and what he said he was going to do to me as soon as I recaptured the tarantula, was only equalled by what he threatened to do to me if I didn't recapture it.

Well, the search in the dormitory was hectic enough, in all conscience, but it was nothing compared to the hunt that took place through the whole house now. I should think it must have been the greatest tarantula hunt ever organised, and scores of inoffensive spiders were put on the spot, but of the tarantula itself no sign or trace could be found.

Macgregor was the first to tumble to the truth, and the Fourth must have been in humour for simply lynching me when he put them wise. They gave up looking for the tarantula there and then, and began a raging man-hunt for little me.

But I had taken good care they wouldn't find me, for in the middle of all the confusion and excitement I had grabbed a couple of blankets and curled myself up inside a huge portmanteau in the box-room, where no one thought of looking for me. I don't know what time they gave it up and went to bed, dead beat; but personally, I slept the sleep of the just for the rest of the night — or the unjust; whichever way you look at it.

As for the occupant of my little box, I never recovered it. Needless to say it wasn't a tarantula, but a harmless white mouse I had made a pet of for weeks past.

The tarantula had been a happy inspiration invented by me on the spur of the moment to give the Fourth something else to think about besides ragging me. And it had succeeded pretty well, for the time being, anyway. Of course, there was the morrow. I wasn't half going to have some explaining to do. But, bless you, as I've hinted before, if it was a habit of mine to worry about tomorrow or the next day, I'd have been snow-white at the age of five.

VIATORS FLYING OVER THE HARA DESERT HAVE TO CARRY CHORS WITH THEM. THIS IS TO LD THEIR AEROPLANES DURING NDSTORMS IF FORCED TO LAND.

IT WILL RULE THE WAVES — THE WIRELESS WAVES. BECAUSE IT IS ONE OF THE FLEET OF BROADCASTING STATION BUOYS THAT AN AMERICAN COMPANY PROPOSES TO ANCHOR AT VARIOUS POINTS IN THE OCEAN.

IT'S A ONE-MAN SUBMARINE. MR. BOLAR OF CALIFORNIA GETS GREAT FUN PILOTING HIS MINIATURE SUBMARINE UNDER WATER WHILE IT IS TOWED BY A MOTOR BOAT.

E MINERS AWAY BACK IN 820 CARRIED THOSE RING-SHAPED WATER-BOTTLES. HEY WERE SO SHAPED TO ENABLE HEM TO BE SLIPPED OVER THE ARM, LEAVING THE HAND FREE TO CARRY TOOLS.

# STRANGE BUT TRUE!

It wasn't only in the classroom that the readers of **ADVENTURE** were treated to facts and figures. Their favourite reading was also packed with snippets of information, but these were fun facts and unlikely to come in handy at exam time.

GAINSBOROUGH, THE ENGLISH PAINTER, SOMETIMES USED BRUSHES WITH SIX-FOOT HANDLES. THIS ENABLED HIM TO SEE THE EFFECT OF HIS STROKES WITHOUT STEPPING BACK FROM THE EASEL.

THESE LITTLE AIR CUSHIONS FOR FITTING ON ELBOWS ARE NOW BEING USED BY TYPISTS TO KEEP THEM FROM GETTING JOINT-ACHE.

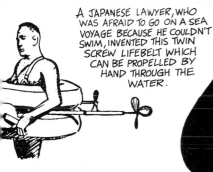

A JAPANESE LAWYER, WHO WAS AFRAID TO GO ON A SEA VOYAGE BECAUSE HE COULDN'T SWIM, INVENTED THIS TWIN SCREW LIFEBELT WHICH CAN BE PROPELLED BY HAND THROUGH THE WATER.

IMAGINE A ROYAL CROWN IN A PAWN SHOP! RICHARD WAS SO HARD UP IN 1386 THAT HE PAWNED HIS CROWN FOR £5,000

JUST THE THING FOR A HEAT-WAVE — A FLOATING JIG-SAW PUZZLE! OF COURSE, THEY CAN ONLY BE USED IN CALM WATER, FOR A WAVE WOULD UNDO HOURS OF WORK.

NESE DUCKS ARE NOT TAKEN TO RKET—INSTEAD THEY TAKE THEIR NERS. ON CHINESE RIVERS, IT IS A MON SIGHT TO SEE A BOAT BEING ED BY DUCKS HARNESSED TO IT.

A FULL-GROWN LION AT LUNA PARK ZOO, U.S.A., IS SO TAME THAT IT IS HARNESSED TO A CART AND TAKES CHILDREN FOR A RIDE.

IN BERLIN YOU NEEDN'T GET WET IN A SUDDEN SHOWER! IN THE STREETS THERE ARE SLOT MACHINES WHICH SUPPLY OIL-PAPER UMBRELLAS WHEN A COIN IS INSERTED.

# Schooldays

# FREE FOR ALL!

As if page after page of thrilling tales wasn't enough, adventure story fans were regularly treated to a free gift in their favourite paper. These giveaways could be anything from a tin jumping frog to a pilot's cap, but the most popular gifts were sets of cards to collect in an album, replica medals or a tiny book full of either facts or funnies.

## THE SKIPPER
— PRICE 2D

Nº 488 · JAN. 6TH 1940

### AIR PILOT'S CAP
FOR EVERY READER

THIS GREAT GIFT GIVEN FREE

NEXT WEEK

# COVER STORY

Schoolboys in the 1930s and '40s probably didn't like school any more than they do today, but they loved school stories and knew where to find them — in the pages of **HOTSPUR**. And these classroom tales provided plenty of eye-catching covers.

THE HOTSPUR

Nº 190 — APRIL 17TH 1937 — EVERY FRIDAY — 2D

OLD TEACHERS NEVER DIE — WORSE LUCK.

THE FIRST-AID SQUAD'S FIRST VICTIM

THE WONDERFUL WIZARD of BOZ

HOTSPUR

Nº 446 — SEPTEMBER 12TH 1942 — PRICE 2D

RED CIRCLE of DEATH

HOTSPUR

Nº 198 — JUNE 12TH — 1937 — EV

DOWN WITH HOME LESSONS

# SCHOOLDAYS

WOOLLY WEST
THE TEACHER WITH
THE WORLD'S
WORST MEMORY

WASH YOUR NECK
FOR DR SANDERS!

THE SECRET
ROUND THE
CIRCUS KID

THE
IRON
TEACHER
SPEAKS

### SLICK    STICK    SMILE

### HAPPY HARRY, THE CAMERA MAN

Years before anyone had heard the names **Dandy** and **Beano,** these early comic stars entertained readers in the pages of **Adventure, Rover** and **Wizard.**

## QUICK SLICK QUIPS

War in the air! War behind enemy lines! . . . In fact almost every kind of conflict provided a theme for adventure stories. Two in particular, 'V for Vengeance' and 'I Flew With Braddock' thrilled readers of *WIZARD* and *ROVER* in the '40s and '50s, then proved their enduring popularity by becoming picture stories in *HORNET* and *VICTOR*.

In the 1970s demand for war fiction was still high. The weekly *WARLORD* became an instant hit when it was launched in 1974, with its long, complete story each week, 'Code-name Warlord'. This introduced readers to the heroic adventures of Lord Peter Flint.

# I FLEW WITH BRADDOCK

Sergeant Matt Braddock, V.C., D.F.M., was one of the R.A.F.'s greatest pilots. His story is told by Sergeant George Bourne, who flew as his navigator. In the late autumn of 1940 the German blitzes were at their worst. The new Beaufighter, with radar equipment (A.I.), was just coming into service in small numbers and Bomber Command supplied some of the crews for these new night fighters. Braddock and Bourne volunteered.

## NIGHT FIGHTER SQUADRON.

FROM the first sight of him, Braddock took a liking to Squadron Leader Caffney, the Commanding Officer of the new night fighter squadron being formed on the partly-completed aerodrome at Whitmere.

Caffney perched himself on the edge of the desk in the draughty hut which served as his office.

"The Beaufighter is fast and it packs a punch but it's rather tricky to handle," he said in his somewhat drawling voice.

"I've flown a Beau," Braddock said gruffly. "It's a good aeroplane when it's handled right."

"I rather care for it myself," Caffney replied. "Have you had any experience of A.I. (Air Interception) equipment?"

"Not yet," I answered.

"The gen is briefly this," Caffney said. "The bandit is picked up by the ground radar stations with their long range. With that information in front of him, the Controller guides the Beaufighter to the bandit and puts it, if he has any luck, within a mile or two of the Hun."

"I understand that," I told him.

"At that range, the radar set in the Beaufighter should start to show the bandit on its screen," said Caffney. "It's then up to the observer — that's you, Bourne — to guide the pilot on to the bandit."

He gave a shrug.

"It sounds simple," he said. "Yet nine times out of ten something seems to go wrong. Teething troubles, of course, but a bit wearing. You'll need heaps of flying by day to get into the way of things."

We left the hut and squelched through the quagmire. One runway had

been completed. Another was being laid down. The permanent buildings were not much above foundation level.

Flight Sergeant Haycock, the radar instructor, was waiting for us. He conducted us to a hut in which there was a model of a Beaufighter cockpit containing the A.I. equipment.

The screen resembled the tube of a small television set. It was surrounded by numerous knobs and dials.

Braddock listened intently while Haycock started his lesson.

"What's the distance at which an enemy aircraft can be picked up by a fighter?" he asked.

"Roughly speaking it depends on the height at which you're flying," Haycock answered. "If you're flying at ten thousand feet, then you'll see the bandit in your screen when it's ten thousand feet away. If you're at eight thousand feet, then you'll detect it at eight thousand."

"Why?" growled Braddock.

"It's because of the reflection of the earth," Haycock replied. "Some of the energy from your transmitter goes straight down, see, and the ground sends back a signal of such strength that it blots out the reflection of the enemy plane. Get it?"

"I get it," said Braddock. "You can't see the enemy in the screen if it's at a greater distance than your own height above the ground."

I've included these few paragraphs of technical conversation just to indicate the difficulty of using the new and complicated equipment devised by British scientists to stop the devastation of our cities.

With the aid of the model, we were able, without leaving the ground, to practise the use of the "eye that could see in the dark."

Under the instruction of Haycock, the six crews at Whitmere put in hours of practice during the next few days.

We lived under primitive conditions and worked hard to learn our new job.

These rough and ready conditions suited Braddock. Mud, cold and draughty huts were things he could put up with.

Squadron Leader Caffney was one of us, living rough as we did and working even harder. The Adjutant, Flight Lieutenant Bob Bryant, kept the administration running smoothly.

We had been on the station a week before the planes became available for practice flights and for learning how to work with the G.C.I. (Ground Control Interception) that would be controlling us.

## RADAR TRY-OUT.

ON a frosty morning I stood by our Beaufighter while Braddock checked over the engines with the fitters.

The Bristol Beaufighter was a burly-looking, two-engined aircraft. It packed a colossal punch with four cannon and six Browning machine-guns. It was painted sooty black with a rough, non-reflecting surface.

I was as padded as an Eskimo, for in those days the Beau had no cockpit heating.

Braddock was finally satisfied, got down and came over to me. The Beau flown by Don Davis was making its approach to land.

It looked all right to me. Davis seemed to be holding off correctly when the machine stalled — lost flying speed abruptly.

The Beau landed with a tremendous crunch and a tyre burst. It skidded off the runway, dipped a wing, which immediately crumpled up like a concertina on the frozen ground and grated to a stop.

The fire tender raced towards it. We started to run as Davis and his observer shot out of the cockpit and jumped to the ground.

They were no worse than shaken and the plane did not catch fire, but would need major repairs before it would fly again.

Caffney had grabbed a rail on the fire tender and ridden out with it. He was having a job to control his feelings.

"It stalled too quickly," Davis said hoarsely. "It didn't give me a chance. It stalled and I flopped, the black beast."

The noise of motors caused us to look round. Martin Jones was returning in his Beau. He very nearly stalled, too. It was touch-and-go for a tense instant. The plane bounced hard but he kept control.

A minute or so later, he came over to look at the damaged aircraft.

"I'm lucky to get back in one piece myself," he said harshly. "My kite's just about unmanageable in a tight turn. The controls went haywire and nothing happened at all when I tried to use the stick. I only got out of it by using the trimmer."

Braddock pulled on his flying-helmet.

"Come on, George," he said. "Let's go!"

We got into the cockpit and shut the cover. The engines were started up and warmed. We taxied on to the runway and, watched by numerous spectators, made a normal take-off.

We climbed to 10,000 feet and it was like sitting on an iceberg with the wind blowing straight from the North Pole. It was a job to manipulate the knobs with my numbed fingers when we started on our tests.

I'd just contacted the G.C.I. station when the light in the screen went out.

"The radar's packed up, Brad," I said into the inter-com.

"Better tell 'em," he growled. "We'll go back to base."

I pressed the button on the radio box and reported to the Controller that the set had packed up. He did not seem surprised.

We lost height swiftly as we headed back for base. Since Braddock did not warn me, I wasn't expecting the sensational manner of his return.

I was rather puzzled admittedly, when we screeched towards the 'drome at no more than two hundred feet.

I snatched a breath when he pulled up in a stall turn, dropped the wheels and flaps and landed the Beau as if it were a single-engined fighter.

Then he gave a gruff chuckle.

"That'll show 'em, George," he said. "It's time they stopped grousing about the Beau."

The other pilots still looked astonished when we left the plane. No comment was made as Braddock strolled in. He'd given a perfect demonstration that the Beau was nothing to be afraid of when it was handled right.

## THE WHISPERING DEATH.

AT about eight o'clock that night, most of us were in the living hut. The stove glowed nearly red hot.

Since there was nobody in the squadron who could give him a real game of darts, Braddock sat reading. Judging by the bucking bronco on the cover of the magazine, it was literature of the Wild West.

Except for the moaning of the east wind, there was silence until a siren wailed in the nearby town of Whitmere.

Braddock dropped the magazine and sat listening. Within a few minutes we heard the sound of German bombers. There was a continuous drone as they flew on a north-westerly course.

Sergeant Tom Kelway got up from his chair.

"It's the Midlands again," he said grimly. "Coventry or Birmingham."

Braddock jumped violently to his feet.

"I can't stand this," he snarled. "Come on, George!"

I grabbed my cap and overcoat and followed him.

It was freezing cold with white frost

glimmering faintly. The stars spangled the night sky.

Braddock broke into a run, heading for the C.O.'s hut. He threw the door open and pushed through the curtains.

Caffney and the Adjutant were together and jerked their heads round at our intrusion.

"Have we got to stay on the ground with this going on?" Braddock demanded, turning a thumb upwards towards the sound. "Why don't we take off and have a smack at 'em?"

"We're not operational, Braddock," Bryant spluttered. "Our crews haven't finished training."

"Then let's go up and get some real practice," retorted Braddock.

"I've been feeling like that myself! Chained lion, you know," Caffney exclaimed. "If Ground Control is operating they may have their hands full already looking after the West Mittering fighters."

"Those dated old Blenheims," barked Braddock, and it was a fact that the Blenheim night-fighters were slower than the bombers they were supposed to catch. "They'll do no good."

He struck a responsive spark from Caffney.

"Bob," he rapped at the Adjutant, "alert the ground crews and armourers for two aircraft, mine and Braddock's. You chaps go and get kitted up while I try and work the oracle —" He grabbed for his phone. "I'll tackle the Air Officer Commanding Group and see what he says. He isn't a stuffy type."

We dashed away from the hut. There was no doubt from the continuous roar that the Germans were delivering a major attack.

"Our C.O.'s a good type," Braddock said as we ran. "He'll work it if we can."

We raced over to our hut and started to get ready. Braddock grinned at me.

"Put your thick socks on, George," he said.

I put on three pairs of socks before ramming my feet into my fleecy flying boots. I stuck on every garment I could find before putting on my flying coat. Braddock was less bulky.

The moment we reached the C.O.'s

hut, we knew the answer. He'd chucked his tunic off and was hauling a heavy sweater over his head.

"The A.O.C. has bitten," he said through the sweater. "Jerry's attacking Manchester. We can take off as soon as we're ready. Marton Control will handle us. Your call-sign will be Nightjar —"

Caffney rapped out the rest of the technical information.

"You'll be taking off first," he said. "Good hunting!"

"Good hunting to you," exclaimed Braddock.

Five minutes later, we were taxi-ing on to the runway. The lights of the flare-path were going to be exposed long enough for us to take off.

Away on the horizon, search-lights were wig-wagging and there was a distant red glow.

In front of me, Braddock's helmeted head and his shoulders were dimly silhouetted against the amber lighting of his instrument panel.

I turned my head and saw the flames spitting from the twin exhausts. We got permission to go and the flare-path twinkled.

Braddock's left hand moved on the throttles and the roar of the motors doubled. We started to roll forward. I saw him nudging the stick forward to get the tail up as we picked up speed. When he pulled it back I knew we were airborne.

We climbed fast with the earth sinking below us and the sky black and vast.

"Hello, Night Jar Two. This is Moonshine Control. Are you receiving?" rasped a voice through the static.

"Go ahead, Moonshine Control, you're loud and clear," Braddock answered.

"I've got a bite for you," the Controller said. "A bandit five miles ahead. Angels Twelve!"

Angels Twelve meant at twelve thousand feet. Braddock flew on the course the Controller gave him and Bourne waited tensely for the word to switch on the plane's radar. At last it came.

"Angels Twelve" meant at twelve thousand feet. Braddock flew on the course the controller gave him and Bourne waited tensely for the word to switch on the plane's radar. At last it came.

Hello, Nightjar Two. This is Moonshine Control. Are you receiving me?

Go ahead, Moonshine Control, you're loud and clear.

I've got a bite for you — A bandit five miles ahead, Angels Twelve!

Hold it now. He's straight ahead and a bit below.

I see him! He's a little to starboard, Brad.

I see it! It's a Dornier! Tally-Ho!

Our guns have jammed! They won't fire!

We'll have to try something else. I'll see if I can scare them with the landing light.

The Beaufighter swooped in for the kill. Braddock pressed the firing button, then . . .

Achtung! Achtung! Achtung!

He's jettisoned his bombs. They shouldn't do much harm here. Well, let's get back to base.

The extinguishers have put the fire out, but the starboard engine's done for!

The port engine's spluttering! It must have got a bullet too! And the wireless is dead! Drop a red flare, George.

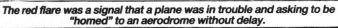

The red flare was a signal that a plane was in trouble and asking to be "homed" to an aerodrome without delay.

Good! Our signal was seen. They're showing a searchlight to guide us to a 'drome.

But we'll never make it. The port engine's about to pack up, or I'm a Dutchman. Time for us to leave, George. Bale out!

I'm stuck! Something must have caught below!

George is stuck! I've got to land this crate!

Both engines useless, the Beaufighter swooped towards the ground, Braddock fighting desperately to keep it on an even keel.

Sergeants Braddock and Bourne report to the commanding officer at once.

Rockner must have arrived! Come on!

In the C.O.'s office, Wing Commander Rockner was sceptical about Braddock's report of the shooting down.

Come, come, Sergeant. You only saw the plane that shot you down for the merest fraction of a second. Surely you could have been mistaken?

No, I couldn't. I saw its silhouette distinctly and the pilot should have identified me. Either his recognition was bad or he'd lost his nerve and was blazing away at anything he saw.

It's stupid to talk like that. At the time of the incident there wasn't another Beau within three miles of you. I wouldn't like to think this was all an excuse for not seeing a German plane till it was too late!

You're not helping me to get this sorted out, sergeant!

I don't make up fancy stories. If a German had shot me up I'd have said so. It was a Beau.

I'm not telling lies to cover up for the chap who shot me down. He's a menace and he'll do the same again if he's not found.

Just a minute, please. I've got some fresh gen. This call came from the officer in charge of the recovery of Braddock's plane. He says that shell fragments and bullets found in the wreck are British! Braddock was right!

Next day, Bourne went for a walk.

What's this thing? Oh I know — it's one of the observer corps' lookout posts.

How long have you been in the observer corps?

I've been in it right from the start of the war.

Look, that Hudson. It's been shuttling back and forward for about an hour now.

You blokes must be hot stuff at aircraft recognition. Tell me, if you got a quick look at a Hudson head-on, could you distinguish it from a Messerschmitt 110?

Yes, I could. There is a certain similarity, but a chap would have to be very green for there to be any confusion between the two.

*Ten minutes later.*

Here comes the Hudson again.

Now there's a Beaufighter. I think it's Rockner.

Hey, it's shooting up the Hudson!

The pilot must have thought it was a Messerschmitt 110!

It's going into the sea! Come on, I've got a boat moored at the inlet.

I hope the crew are all right.

It's unlikely. The Hudson went down steeply.

*A few minutes later.*

Well, this is where it went down. Any sign of life?

There's a man hanging on to that buoy.

Easy does it, old chap. You're safe now.

We'd better get back. There are no more survivors.

A Beaufighter got us — one of our own planes!

A plane lost and four men dead — and all because a trigger-happy prune didn't know his aircraft recognition!

*After the rescued man had been taken to hospital, Bourne returned to the aerodrome and went straight to the intelligence room.*

Ah, Bourne. We've heard about the Hudson and your part in the rescue. Can you fill in any more details?

I'll try to, sir. But can you tell me something first. Has Rockner come back from his patrol, and have his guns been fired?

That was Rockner. I saw the single Swastika on his Beau's nose.

Well, Rockner's hopped it now. Hey, where's Jerry? We've lost him!

He must have gone down among the marshes. I'll tell the controller, then we'll land at Birling.

Why Birling? We could get home all right.

It's got to be Birling. I've got an idea.

Twenty minutes later, Braddock put the Beaufighter down at Birling airfield.

I'm the flying control officer here. Had a bit of a dust-up?

Yes, we were in a fight with a Messerschmitt. I don't think she hit anything vital, but I'd just like to make sure.

Very wise. Look — there are some bullet-holes in the tail. I'll have the plane checked over. Meanwhile, I suppose you could do with a cup of tea?

Thank you, sir. But first, I'd better phone East Saltney and tell them where we are.

Brad's taking a long time.

While Braddock went to phone, Bourne was taken to the sergeants' mess.

I've been doing a bit of scouting, George, I've been talking to the Sergeant Armourer. On the afternoon the Hudson was shot down, Rockner landed here. And listen to this — his guns had been used!

He asked for the gun magazines to be reloaded. No questions were asked, of course, as he's a high-ranking officer. The guns were loaded and the usual fabric pasted over them.

Well, you've got him where you want him now.

Yes! But we still don't have any proof! But I think I know how to change that!

So, next day—

Hullo, Brad. Hey, what's the flying kit for? Have they found another plane for us?

No, they haven't. I'm going to fly as Rockner's observer — only he doesn't know it yet.

I've got an idea to catch Rockner out. I've made one or two alterations to his plane. Now I need your help. Bring a cushion and I'll tell you what I want you to do.

Braddock led Bourne to a spot near Rockner's Beaufighter.

Here come Rockner and Hatherly now. Are you ready?

I hope your plan works, or we're really in trouble.

Plane ready for take-off, sir.

Good. Carry on with the drill.

That's Rockner inside. Now's my chance.

Ugh!

Right, Brad, now!

This is it!

Okay, Hatherly, you can relax. I'll let you up now.

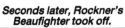

Seconds later, Rockner's Beaufighter took off.

Almost as soon as the plane was in its patrol area, the radar controller called it up.

Hello, searcher one. Hostile planes are approaching the Humber. Your course is Zero Four Five Degrees, Angels Ten.

We're on our way!

Let's hope for some good hunting, Hatherly. You'd better get to your radar set.

Yes, sir.

Rockner had no suspicion that Braddock was his observer as voices over the plane's intercom system were unrecognisable.

Hello, Searcher One. There is an aircraft four miles in front. Identify and challenge.

As soon as they were within range of the small A.I. radar set the Beaufighter carried, Braddock took over from the controller.

Aircraft slightly to port and below.

I see it! I'll give him it in the guts!

Blast! The guns have jammed! Wait till I see the armourer about this!

We might as well head for home.

When the Beaufighter landed, Squadron Leader Jenson, Rockner's second-in-command, was there to meet it.

Here's the C.O. now.

You went without Hatherly, sir!

What! Then who flew with me?

I did. I saved the lives of some of our blokes by altering the gunswitch of your Beau. The plane you were going to shoot down was a Wellington!

You're under arrest for tampering with an aircraft. As for the plane being a Wellington I identified it clearly as a Heinkel!

You were carrying a camera tonight, and that was a photo flash you let off when you squeezed the button. I fixed that, too! You'll see that the plane was a Wellington, and so will others!

I don't care if I do get my knuckles rapped over this, Rockner — but you're finished with flying!

Next day.

There goes Rockner now, Brad. The brass hats acted quickly when they saw that photo of the Wellington.

Yes. Now Rockner is posted and grounded, we can get on with winning the war!

# SIGNS OF THE TIMES

It took more than Hitler and his henchmen to stop Britain's schoolboys enjoying their favourite reading. During World War II, publications like **ROVER, WIZARD** and *ADVENTURE* continued to appear, but their adverts for bicycle lamps and pocket watches were replaced by the ones opposite.

Flint jumped—

Let's hope the branches will bear my weight!

Flint leaped from the tree on to a rock face, and, ignoring the 2000 foot drop, began the perilous climb.

Once over the ridge I'll be on the North Slope. There's a ski hut there.

But, when he reached the slope —

Oh-oh! Someone's shooting at me again — but I must make it to the ski-hut.

Flint "borrowed" skis and made his escape —

Ach! The Englander is getting away!

Just in time! Off we go!

I'll make for the airfield at Muur and try to find a plane to get me out of here.

Flint reached the airfield perimeter.

I'll just climb the fence and . . . Oops! I've startled that hare.

No more snow, so I'll have to leg it the rest of the way. Still, it's only a couple of miles now.

The frightened animal ran wildly into the fence —

What —? The fence is electrified!

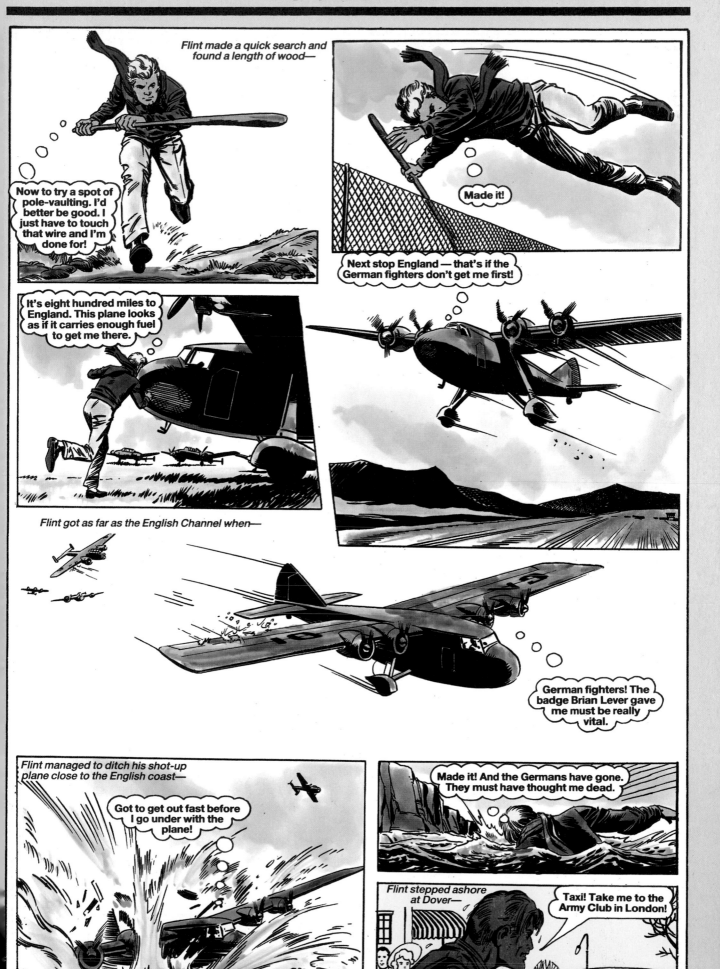

Good afternoon, Sergeant. Is General Ferguss here?

He is, my Lord.

Greetings, General. Brian Lever asked me to give you this badge. He couldn't make it himself.

The badge! Quickly, tell me what happened, Flint!

Next day, Flint returned to his ancestral home —

That was an interesting chat with the General. I think I'll do what he wants.

Two days later, Lord Flint gave a dinner party—

The Germans have invaded Poland. That means war now. I suppose you'll be joining the Guards, Flint?

All that shooting and fighting! No — not for me, thanks.

Britain declared war on Germany, but Lord Flint decided to shoot on his estate. Then he received a mysterious summons to the Army club.

The dinner party broke up abruptly!

Take this white feather, Lord Flint — the sign of cowardice.

My thanks, Lady Bencham. I'll wear it especially for you.

News of his cowardice had spread.

Evening, Sergeant. You look very smart in your new uniform.

I'm proud to serve my country — not like some I know!

Flint was shown into a private room—

General Ferguss told me you risked your life to bring this badge back, Flint. It was a great help — but we need you again.

So that's why the General told me not to join up. You want me for some kind of secret work!

# Code-name WARLORD

Yes. The badge has the date of the German invasion of Poland on it. That helped us to make vital preparations. But there was something else . . .

Yes, Brian mentioned a piece of metal. It must be somewhere in the wreck of his car. I'll bring it back, sir.

I knew I could rely on you. The arrangements have all been made. Good luck!

That night—

There's my plane . . . once this secret mission is over I'll join the Guards and clear my name.

Four hours later, Flint floated down into Austria.

The old castle I own is near here. Josef, the caretaker, will help me.

But when Flint landed—

Halt! Hande hoch!

Sorry, old chap. Can't stay to argue!

As dawn broke, Flint reached the spot where Lever was shot.

The car's gone. But where? I'll speak to Josef.

The Nazi flag! The Germans have taken over my castle.

So I'll have to use the back entrance!

# Code-name WARLORD

THAT'S WHERE THE ACTION'S FOUND DURING WARTIME . . . AND THAT WAS DEFINITELY THE CASE WHEN IT CAME TO **ROVER, SKIPPER, ADVENTURE** AND **HOTSPUR.** THOSE PUBLICATIONS' COVERS WERE ALWAYS THEIR MOST EYE-CATCHING, ACTION-PACKED PAGES.

FRONT

# V FOR VENGEANCE

> **'V FOR VENGEANCE'** was the motto of The Deathless Men, underground fighters who had escaped from German prison camps during World War II to wage a war of vengeance and terror against the top Nazis. The story below appeared in *WIZARD* in 1942.

The big blue saloon slowed as it passed the entrance to the Tuileries Gardens in Paris. Even though it was two o'clock in the morning, and the car carried Otto Leben, Chief of the Gestapo in Paris, the German chauffeur obeyed the red warning of the traffic lights.

Not for more than a few seconds was the car held up, then the lights changed to green, and it glided forward, yet during those few seconds the door on the off-side had opened softly and a huddled figure jumped out into the road, rolled over then rose quickly and silently.

This figure slipped swiftly through the entrance to the gardens, so grey and indistinct, with a shabby grey suit, grey felt hat, and grey-masked face. There were grey gloves on his hands, and on his feet grey rubber shoes. He merged into the shadows beneath the archway, and vanished.

The blue saloon reached the Place de la Concorde, stopping at the Gestapo headquarters.

Black-uniformed sentries came smartly to attention. The chauffeur alighted from his seat and jerked the door open on the side nearest the steps.

"We have arrived, Herr Leben," he informed the uniformed figure inside.

There was neither sound nor movement from the Chief of the Gestapo. The chauffeur glanced swiftly at the impassive sentries, then leaned inside and shook his passenger gently.

The figure toppled sideways. Herr Leben, the Butcher of Paris, was quite dead. Pinned to his chest was a slip of paper which was carried inside to be read.

At the head of the page was a blood-red letter V, fully two inches high, and underneath this there was printed in German:

"V for VENGEANCE. The free peoples of Europe strike again. This rat is only one of many who will die. The Deathless Men are answering the heart-rendering cries of the innocent sufferers. It is now the turn of the tyrants, the murderers, the torturers, to tremble. Before long, all the following will share the fate of this scum. They cannot escape us. Their time is coming."

Then followed a long list of names and members of the Gestapo, and Nazi officials of various ranks, finishing up with the final three — Goebbels, Goering and Hitler.

The name of Otto Leben was at the top, but it had already been crossed off with a thick red line!

Consternation and rage showed in the faces of the Nazis. Leben's second-in-command roared for the chauffeur to be brought in.

"Well?" demanded the new chief. "Who else was with you?"

"No one," replied the chauffeur nervously, "I was alone! There was just Herr Leben and myself!"

"Then you killed Herr Leben, eh?"

"No, no, no!" shrieked the prisoner. "I did not touch him. I'm a good Nazi."

"Take him into the cellar and refresh his memory!" snapped the second-in-command to the burly troopers.

"Do we know anything about any society calling themselves The Deathless Men?" demanded the acting chief.

"No, sir. I have never heard the name before," replied his lieutenant.

"Get me General Konrad on the phone at once. We must report this to him. There will have to be reprisals. As Governor of Paris it is his duty to order the arrest of hostages. Paris will tremble before we've finished."

His eyes ran down the list of names on the paper before him. Immediately below that of Herr Leben he saw that of General Konrad, Governor of Paris!

"And what about Von Reich?" asked someone. "He is staying at the Crillon. Shall we phone him as well?"

"No, let him finish his sleep in peace. It will be bad enough to tell him in the morning. When he makes his report on this to Himmler, we can all expect to fry!"

Whispers of what had happened, and of the threat of the Deathless Men, spread through the city. Who were the Deathless Men? asked everyone. Who was their leader?

The same question was being asked in a palatial suite at the Crillon Hotel, where Von Reich, second only to

Himmler in the Black Guards, stormed and raved at the local Gestapo officials.

"What is this gang of Deathless Men?" he thundered. "Find them! Find out who is their leader, then we shall get somewhere. Find out or I'll name you personally in my report."

The crestfallen officials fled to pursue their inquiries. But there was no result. The following midnight found gaunt-faced officers and police officials standing round the desk of General Konrad, the brutal Governor of Paris.

"What are we going to do now, General?" asked someone.

"This!" General Konrad reached for a long, typewritten list lying beside him. "Here we have the names of the two hundred hostages detained since this morning."

After counting them he drew a thick line under the fiftieth name, and signed his initials at the top. "Shoot all those whose names are above that line. If that doesn't bring these Parisians to their senses, we'll shoot another fifty the following morning. Goodnight, gentlemen. I'm going to bed."

They clicked their heels as he rose, and the commandant in charge of the prison departed with the list of doomed hostages, five of whom were women.

General Konrad passed two sets of dormitories before he reached the big apartment where he usually slept. It was furnished in palatial fashion, some of the finest antique furniture in Paris having been seized and brought there.

The last sound he heard after he had put out the light and had climbed into bed was the compelling footsteps of the sentry in the corridor outside.

There was a slight creaking noise in the corner of the room where the door of a huge, carved wardrobe was opening. It opened slowly, there was a rustle, and a figure stepped softly on to the plushly-carpeted floor.

Little light came in through the curtains over the window, but there was sufficient to show the shape as that of a man, tall but rather stooping, dressed entirely in grey, with grey felt hat, grey mask covering his face, grey gloves and rubber-soled shoes of the same colour.

As silently as a shadow the grey man approached the bed. In one hand he had a long, narrow dagger, no thicker than a pencil.

Carefully he bent over the general, and shone a small flashlamp upon the coarse face. The light disturbed the sleeper. He grunted, and flung out his arm.

The German's eyelids twitched. The light was disturbing him. Finally it wakened him. He opened his eyes for a moment, blinked furiously, hardly knowing whether he was awake or asleep, and glimpsed a shapeless grey face bending over him.

He opened his mouth to shout, but no sound came. The dagger point had descended swiftly. His big body gave a twist, then lay still.

The grey man left the dagger where it was. The gloved hands had left no finger-prints on the smooth hilt. From somewhere he produced a slip of paper, which he carefully pinned to the general's pyjama jacket.

It was a copy of the document found on Herr Leben, except that in addition to Herr Leben's name, that of General

# V for VENGEANCE

Konrad was crossed out with a thick line!

As silently as he had approached the bed, the grey intruder crossed to the window where a drainpipe went down two storeys to the ground below.

Gripping the pipe with gloved hands and rubber-soled feet, he swiftly descended to ground level.

The grey man landed lightly, sprinted across the street before the moon came out, and entered a darker street.

He was making for a more crowded quarter of the town, and whenever he heard a car approach or the footfalls of a patrol, he doubled into the shadows and remained still until they had passed. His dark grey colour scheme merged in perfectly on these occasions. No one challenged him until he had almost reached his destination.

Then his luck failed. Turning a corner after listening intently to make sure there was no movement in the street beyond, he ran straight into a German soldier who was standing beside a broken-down lorry.

The grey man ducked and turned for the corner. The weapon in the German's hand barked twice, and the second shot passed through the runner's back, close to his spine. It spun him against the wall, which he clutched with both hands to prevent himself from falling.

A gasp came from behind the mask. His knees seemed to be doubling under him, but he held himself erect, while at the same time feeling for a small but efficient revolver which was in his side-pocket.

The Nazi was shouting at the top of his voice as he ran up to finish off his victim. They both fired at once, there being barely a second between the shots. The German's shot smashed into the man's stomach, but the solitary bullet fired by the crouching figure dropped him dead on the pavement.

The grey-clad man went down on one knee, coughed, clutched his stomach, then heard running feet and many shouts. Patrols were coming. In a few moments that quarter of Paris would be roused and cordoned off.

He hauled himself erect once more, and felt his way round the corner. Twice he fell, but each time he rose to his feet to stagger another few steps, until he finally crossed the road to a public telephone box which he had seen there.

The Germans had not reached the body of the soldier on the pavement around the corner. Whistles were blowing, motor-cycles were speeding to the spot. The man-hunt was up, and the victim they sought was fighting against unconsciousness as he listened to the ringing of the bell at the other end.

The telephone bell rang at the bedside of Von Reich, in his bedroom at the Crillon Hotel. Sleepily, the dark man with the bushy eyebrows reached for the receiver.

"Ja!" he said cautiously.

"Is that Von Reich?"

"Ja! What do you want?" The second-in-command of the Black Guard spoke in a low voice. "Who is it?"

"This is Jack Twelve. It — it is done."

The man who had called himself Jack Twelve managed to get forty yards from the phone box before he collapsed. There he lay for five minutes longer before the German motor-cyclists found him and roughly lifted him to shine a light on his masked face.

He was dead.

At the headquarters of the Gestapo in Paris the new chief licked dry lips as he listened to the tirade launched at him by Von Reich.

It was the morning of the discovery that General Konrad had been murdered in his bed, and of the finding of a grey-clad man dead in the Rue de Chaume.

". . . If you can't even protect the Governor of Paris you're not fit to hold your job!" Von Reich was roaring. "What is the Gestapo for? What good are you if you don't do your duty? I suppose you've found out nothing about the man shot in the street?"

"Ja, we have done that," grunted the new chief, clenching his hands in temper. "His name is Kouniz — Johan Kouniz, and he is a Czech, a native of Prague."

"Is anything known about him?" snapped Von Reich, his eyebrows and moustache bristling.

"Ja, in 1939, when we took over Czechoslovakia, he was arrested as a suspected person and sent to Germany to the Buchenwald concentration camp. There he stubbornly refused to give any information about his late friends and colleagues. He was submitted to a course of 'softening', but it did not produce worthwhile results. His face was so — er — altered by the handling of his questioners that he usually wore a handkerchief over it when mixing with the other prisoners afterwards. Maybe that's why he wore a mask when we found him."

"How did he come to be here in Paris?" thundered Von Reich.

"That we do not know. According to records phoned from Germany half an hour ago, Johann Kouniz died and was buried at Buchenwald nine months ago."

Von Reich jerked as though with astonishment.

"Dead, buried and then here in Paris!" He pointed at the paper taken from the chest of General Konrad. "I'm certain he was one of those Deathless Men, and I don't like it. Follow up every clue about this Kouniz. Leave no stone unturned. Life is no longer safe here in Paris. What happened about those fifty hostages?"

"They were shot at dawn," was the grim reply. "Tomorrow at dawn a hundred more will die unless the killers of both Leben and Konrad are caught."

"I believe you already have the killer in that Kouniz. Who signs the order for the shooting of the other hundred?"

"General Henkell arrives by plane from Strasbourg at mid-day to take over the Governship of Paris. He will sign the order this evening, I've no doubt. You are going, Herr Von Reich?"

"Yes, I have to compile a report for Berlin in code, and that always takes me some time. I'll be very glad if you'll have half a dozen extra guards put on me after this."

"Certainly!" replied the other.

Through the window he watched Von Reich enter his car and drive away. He would have been more surprised if he could have seen the code message which Von Reich compiled half an hour later in his apartment at the Crillon.

The code used was not that of the German Gestapo, but one of the many used by the British Secret Service. On the face of it the message was in French, and referred to the commandeering of a certain powerful car belonging to the Compte Duval, which was now stored at a garage in the Bois de Boulogne.

Von Reich rang a bell and handed the note to an orderly.

"Send a motor-cyclist with this at once. Tell him to tell that thick-headed patron of the garage that if the car isn't ready for us to take away by six o'clock this evening, I'll land him in prison!"

The message was duly handed to the bearded Frenchman who managed the garage in question.

The Frenchman drew a greasy hand across his face, and tore the envelope open. His face grew more and more surly as he read the imperious message, then he growled:

"Have no fear, it will be done!"

The German returned with this assurance. The garage proprietor wiped his hands on a piece of waste, then entered his office, closing the door behind him. It was a dingy little office, but there was a low cupboard in one corner. Opening the door of this, he stooped and crawled inside. There was a trap-door in the floor, which he raised, descending by a ladder to a small cellar which even the employees of the garage did not know was there.

There was not much in the cellar, but a small telephone instrument hung on the wall. It was of the old-fashioned variety, and was not connected with any of the Paris exchanges, being on a private line.

Monsieur Michenot wound vigorously at the handle, then raised the mouthpiece to speak softly.

"Is that you, Paul? Michenot speaking. I've just had a message from Gregson. It's urgent. He says you are to pass on the word that General Henkell arrives at Le Bourget aerodrome at mid-day from Strasbourg to take over the Governship of Paris. One of his first duties will be to sign for the execution of another hundred hostages tomorrow. Gregson says Henkell's name is not on the list, but it must be added at once, and he must be dealt with before he can sign his name. That is all."

He hung up and returned to his office the way he had come, closing the cupboard door carefully after he had emerged.

Then he sat down at his desk to go through the various requisitioning orders which the Nazis had served to him during the past week. His mind was not on his work. Pierre Michenot, one-time of the French Intelligence, was thinking what a remarkably dangerous job Aylmer Gregson had when posing as Von Reich!

Michenot was one of the very few men in Paris who knew Herr Von Reich was a British Secret Service man who had been "planted" in the Nazi party long before the war.

On the inside of the Nazi councils, trusted by Nazi heads, hated by Nazi underlings, Aylmer Gregson had one of the most important jobs in the war.

**The Deathless Men lived up to their name, when 'V for VENGEANCE' appeared again as a picture story in _HORNET_, 1965.**

There is our first objective, that anti-aircraft warning and defence post.

*The Deathless Men had selected as their next victim, Baron von Bierber, the brutal Nazi Minister for the Re-Education of Occupied Europe. Von Bierber was holding a party at his strongly guarded lakeside villa in the Berlin outskirts.*

*Inside the air-raid post.*

Do you hear the music from the villa? They're having a fine time, I'll bet.

I wish we were doing the same.

*In quick, silent, deadly fashion the Deathless Men overcame the Nazi soldiers.*

There are the levers that work the siren, Jack Four.

Good. Go ahead, Jack Twenty-two.

*Meanwhile, inside the villa . . .*

That's the siren sounding the air raid alert.

Good, that's part two of our plan put into operation. Let's get out of here and carry out the rest.

Listen, Baron Von Bierber — the siren — it is an air raid.

There is nothing to fear. I have one of the deepest shelters in Berlin. It has an interior entrance as well as an outside one. Come, everyone, I will lead the way.

When that canister explodes, it ought to stir things up a bit.

Right, let's head for Von Bierber's shelter.

That was a bomb!

It sounded very close! We must be in the target area!

Don't panic! In a few seconds we'll be safe in the shelter. There are only a few more steps, then a long corridor.

# V for VENGEANCE

The Deathless Men took cover.

But the party about to start was one the Nazis would not enjoy. Click! Every light in the shelter suddenly went out. Many guests cried out, but their shouts were muted into gasps of fear as half a dozen dazzling shafts of torchlight stabbed into the frightened crowd and focussed on the faces of Von Bierber, Fritz Frisch, Count Von Eltz, Hans Kotz, Karl Stump and Franz Speer, six leading Nazis guilty of war crimes.

The torches were held by the Deathless Men.

Vengeance carried out, the Deathless Men slipped away from the panic in the shelter. Behind them, they left the bodies of their six victims.

At the shelter's inside door, arriving Nazi officers were met by terrified fleeing guests.

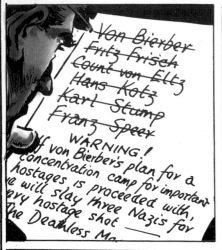

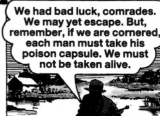

Here come the Nazis, comrades — in a launch. Row harder, we are not far from the other bank.

But even as the avengers fired back at the launch, motor-cycle troops sped along the shore to cut off the last line of retreat.

It's no use, comrades. There are too many against us.

We'll get into the chalet and make our last stand there.

The door is open, Jack Four!

Here comrades, we fight to our last bullet, then die!

And fight they did. The Nazis, attacking from all sides, were met by a blistering fire . . .

Back, men, and take cover! We'll cordon the chalet till reinforcements arrive.

In answer to the call for reinforcements, Colonel Von Reich was sent from Berlin with a hundred Gestapo troopers.

This is going to be tricky but I must find some way to help the Deathless Men if possible.

Colonel, now that your men have arrived, we can rush the chalet and wipe out these Deathless Men.

No! Herr Himmler insists some must be taken alive for interrogation. Cease firing on the left-hand side. I will crawl forward alone and reconnoitre the position.

These Nazis think I'm either a fool or a hero for crawling alone into range of the Deathless Men's fire. They don't know it's the only way I can get in touch with my men to help them if I can.

# WAR

I'm almost there!

Don't shoot! This is Jack One! How many of you are left?

This is Jack Four. There are only five of us left unwounded, Jack One. We have no chance of escape now.

Himmler sent me to take you alive, Jack Four. I must fail, but, if it appears to be my fault, it will be the end of me and our anti-Nazi campaign.

The campaign must go on, Jack One. Do not let our lives stand in the way. Go back and drive the Gestapo in to take us. We will die but no blame will be attached to you.

When you attack, place yourself on the north side, Jack One. We won't fire in that direction.

Thank you, Jack Four. You shall not die in vain!

*Von Reich crawled back to the waiting Gestapo troops.*

There are only a handful of the Deathless Men. A sudden, swift rush on the chalet from all sides and we can take them alive. I will lead the attack from the north side and you three on the east, south and west.

Straight for the chalet! Let no man hold back!

Inside quickly, men! Seize them before they can take poison!

We are too late! I have examined them all. They are all dead, some from bullet wounds but most from poison.

They have beaten us again — and killed over thirty of our men into the bargain! Herr Himmler will be furious!

But Himmler could find no excuse to blame Von Reich. Instead, Von Reich was told to be ready to guard Herr Lutze, head of the Nazi Storm Troopers, who was due in Berlin on a secret visit. Von Reich determined that Lutze, a monster of cruelty, should never reach Berlin alive. He knew when Lutze was due, but not which of two parallel roads he would be using. So Von Reich secretly ordered Jack Ten to wait at one road and Jack Fourteen at the other.

That's Lutze's car now!

Lutze's car was specially armoured, but Jack Ten's bomb was a powerful one.

That will settle Lutze. V for Vengeance!

No man could have lived through that.

But the survivors of Lutze's escort fired on Jack Ten.

We've wounded him! Get after him — and take him alive!

Hearing the explosion of Jack Ten's bombs and the sound of shots, Jack Fourteen had left the parallel road to hurry to his colleague's aid.

Jack Ten is wounded.

Hold on, Jack Ten!

I can hear more storm troopers coming through the wood. I will be ready for them.

No, Jack Fourteen. You can do nothing for me. Your duty is to escape and report to Jack One that Lutze is dead.

Go before they see you, Jack Fourteen. They do not know there are two of us. I'll take this poison capsule. They'll find me dead and look no further. Go! Hurry!

CARL LUTZE

V for VENGEANCE!

Very well, Jack Ten.

But a few minutes later—

Jack Fourteen, come back and kill me! They've shot the poison capsule out of my hand! Don't let them take me alive!

I cannot let Jack Ten be taken and tortured by these fiends!

You cannot be made to talk now, old friend, and your death is avenged. V for Vengeance!

Jack Fourteen silently slipped to the edge of the wood.

Now if I can only get away in that car —

It is one of the Deathless Men. Halt!

I will soon be out of range.

I'll head for Gestapo headquarters in the outskirts of Berlin. Von Reich — Jack One — will be there.

At seventy miles an hour, the car sped through the outskirts of Berlin.

Soon Jack Fourteen pulled up outside the Gestapo headquarters.

V for Vengeance! Lutze is dead and your turn is coming, Von Reich!

Seize him! Take him alive! He is one of the Deathless Men!

You will never take me alive!

A detachment of Gestapo troopers appeared at the double round the corner . . .

Death to the Gestapo!

Time to bite on my poison capsule.

AAGH!

We want that man alive. Let me through to him.

Jack Fourteen lived only long enough to hear these whispered words from his leader.

Well done, comrade.

He is dead. He has taken poison. Are we never going to take one of them alive?

# The War - In Pictures

ELECTRIC CAMERA WORKED BY THE PHOTOGRAPHER IN THE NOSE.

BOMB AIMER AND PHOTOGRAPHER AT SIGHTS OF CAMERA.

SINCE THE OUTBREAK OF WAR THOUSANDS OF VERY VALUABLE PHOTOGRAPHS OF GERMAN TERRITORY HAVE BEEN TAKEN BY R.A.F. PLANES. OUR DIAGRAM SHOWS HOW THESE PHOTOGRAPHS ARE TAKEN BY ELECTRICAL CAMERAS, WORKED BY THE BOMB AIMER AND PHOTOGRAPHER, WHO LIES IN THE NOSE OF THE PLANE. A SURVEY OF GREAT STRETCHES OF LAND CAN BE TAKEN IN SECTIONS BY OVERLAPPING PHOTOGRAPHS. THE PHOTOGRAPHS ARE THEN TRIMMED AND PIECED TOGETHER.

# WISHBONE WUZZY JOINS THE ARMY!

Important plans the Nazis read
But Wuz is there, they'd best take heed.

HAND DER PLANS TO ME!

Adolf speaks, with outstretched hand.
"Giff me der plans," is his command.

THANKS ADOLF!

Addie then gives plans to Wuz.
Shows you what the Wishbone does.

I WISH THERE WAS A DOOR IN THIS SHELL!

TO THE FRONT

Wuz the plans must get home quick.
Makes the Wishbone do the trick.

To France "With Love" huge
shell is sent.
But where is Wuz and document.

THE PLANS COLONEL!

Out pops Wuz from shell's interior.
Hands the plans to his superior.

# THE TIMES

There wasn't a single aspect of life in Britain that wasn't touched by the impact of the Second World War. Schoolboys continued to read adventure stories but the villains were often Nazis and the pages of useful hints which had originally appeared in peacetime now had a more serious message. Even the snappy messages along the tops of pages waged war against the enemy.

A PARVENE IS A TORPEDO-SHAPED DEVICE FOR SWEEPING MINES!

A BARRAGE BALLOON COSTS OVER £500

63 members of parliament are serving in the army!

A MOTOR TORPEDO BOAT COSTS £23,000!

H.M.S. ROYAL SOVEREIGN IS NICK-NAMED THE 'TIDDLEY QUID'!

## HOW A BOY CAN HELP TO WIN THE WAR

Most Adventure readers will be too young to join the "Parashots."

Here are a few suggestions from the Editor for those who want to do their bit in beating Hitler.

ALWAYS KEEP YOUR EYES AND EARS OPEN. DON'T GO PRYING INTO OTHER PEOPLE'S BUSINESS. BUT IF YOU SHOULD HEAR OR SEE ANYTHING SUSPICIOUS DON'T BE AFRAID TO TELL THE POLICE OR THE MILITARY.

YOU ALL KNOW HOW DANGEROUS RUMOURS ARE. YOU WILL BE DOING A SERVICE TO YOUR COUNTRY IF YOU BECOME A SILENT "COLUMNIST" AND DO YOUR BEST TO STOP "CHATTERBUGS."

MANY WASTE MATERIALS ARE OF GREAT VALUE TO THE COUNTRY. YOU CAN HELP THE WAR EFFORT BY COLLECTING ALL THE WASTE PAPER, OLD IRON, ALUMINIUM ETC, YOU CAN.

BUY NATIONAL SAVING CERTIFICATES

THERE IS SURE TO BE A NATIONAL SAVINGS CERTIFICATE SCHEME IN YOUR SCHOOL. IF YOU ARE NOT ALREADY A MEMBER, YOU SHOULD JOIN AT ONCE, EVERY PENNY YOU SAVE WILL HELP TO BEAT THE NAZIS.

WHEN YOU HEAR THE SIRENS, TRY TO BE AN EXAMPLE TO OTHERS BY GOING TO YOUR SHELTER AT ONCE AND STAYING THERE TILL YOU HEAR THE ALL CLEAR. TRY TO HELP OTHERS TO KEEP AS CALM AS POSSIBLE.

NO ADMITTANCE BY ORDER.

NEVER INTERFERE WITH SOLDIERS ON GUARD. THEY HAVE THEIR DUTIES TO PERFORM AND IF YOU SPEAK TO THEM YOU MAY TAKE THEIR MINDS FROM THEIR WORK.

AFTER AN AIR-RAID, IF THERE HAS BEEN MUCH DAMAGE DONE, BOYS MAY BE OF GREAT VALUE AS MESSENGERS. TRY TO MAKE YOUR-SELF AS USEFUL AS POSSIBLE.

# ALL GOOD SPORTS . . .

Sports stories have always been popular in the boys' papers, but surprisingly, one of the most successful didn't feature football, boxing or any of the other exciting spectator sports. In **HORNET'S** Cast Hook and Strike, young Joe Dodds was a mad-keen angler who caught the readers' attention during the 1970s.

And when it came to football, one of the best-loved heroes was no human dynamo. Georgeous Gus had a cannonball shot but didn't believe in running. Readers of **WIZARD**, and later **VICTOR**, also discovered he was a lord and the only player in the league with his own butler.

# GORGEOUS GUS

WHO ARE YOU, AND WHAT ARE YOU DOING HERE? CAN'T YOU SEE I'M BUSY?

MR HOPKINS, I PRESUME. MY CARD, SIR.

**R**EDBURN ROVERS had never had such a disastrous start to the season. They had lost their first four games and failed to score a single goal! Sam Hopkins, the Rovers' manager, was racking his brain one Wednesday morning, trying to pick a team, when he had an unusual visitor.

LOOK, MR JENKINS. I'M A VERY BUSY MAN. I'VE A TEAM TO PICK FOR SATURDAY, AND —

THAT'S WHAT THE MASTER SENT ME HERE FOR. HE WATCHED THE TEAM ON SATURDAY, AND WISHES TO SEE THESE PEOPLE IN THE SIDE — JOE PRATT OF WESTON IN GOAL, DUNCAN AND POWER OF RANGERS AS BACKS, CRUMP OF WOOLFORD AT CENTRE-HALF, MORGAN OF ABERCROM ON THE RIGHT WING, CARTON OF REDPOOL AT INSIDE RIGHT, AND KELLY OF WESTPORT AT INSIDE LEFT.

AND SO WOULD I LIKE TO SEE THEM IN THE TEAM. THEY ARE ALL INTERNATIONALS! AND NO POSHED-UP FLUNKEY'S GONG TO TAKE THE MICKEY OUT OF ME!

NOW DON'T BE HASTY, MR HOPKINS.

I'M NOT GOING TO BE HASTY, CHUM, I'M GOING TO TAKE MY TIME AND ENJOY THIS.

BEFORE YOU RESORT TO FISTICUFFS, I SUGGEST YOU LOOK OUT OF THE WINDOW. I SEE IT IS TEN O'CLOCK, THE TIME WHEN THE PLAYERS SHOULD BE REPORTING.

SEE!

THERE'S DUNCAN, POWERS, CARTON, KELLY — THEY'RE ALL HERE! WHAT'S GOING ON?

THE MASTER HAS BOUGHT THE CLUB AND ARRANGED THE TRANSFERS. HIS ORDERS ARE THAT MARTIN, DODD AND WEBB WILL KEEP THEIR PLACES IN THE TEAM. THE CENTRE-FORWARD POSITION WILL BE KEPT VACANT MEANTIME.

BUT THESE TRANSFERS ALONE MUST HAVE COST A QUARTER OF A MILLION QUID!

MONEY DOESN'T MATTER TO THE MASTER. ONE MORE THING. HE HAS DECIDED THAT AN ADDITION MUST BE MADE TO THE GRANDSTAND. WORKMEN WILL WORK NIGHT AND DAY TO COMPLETE IT.

THE MASTER?

WHO ON EARTH IS THE MASTER?

The whole of Redburn was amazed at the news of the Rovers' signings.

COO, BERT, WHAT A TEAM! RECKON I'LL BE AT THE MATCH. YOU COMING?

TRANSFER SENSATION

ROVERS' FANTASTIC BUYING SPREE. STAR STUDDED TEAM TO MEET CITY ON SATURDAY. WHO IS THE MYSTERY MASTER?

TRY AND STOP ME, MATE!

Workmen toiled night and day, erecting an addition to the stand, a luxurious one-man dressing-room, fitted with all the latest devices and richly furnished. No expense was spared. This ornate building was promptly nicknamed the Royal Pavilion. Meanwhile, football fever swept Redburn. Then at last came Saturday and the chance to see their star-studded team in action.

Rovers won the toss and chose to play with the wind. City kicked off . . .

. . . And the immaculate Rovers centre-forward appeared to lose interest.

# FOOTBALL FACT FILE ...

## WE ARE UNITED

This is the 1985 Milk Cup winning team, managed by Joe Pearson. Success came in the club's centenary year in the pages of CHAMP. Big name transfers from other publications undoubtedly contributed to the victory. Goalie 'Iron' Barr was signed from ROVER and HOTSPUR'S 'Limp Along' Leslie also joined the team.

## STARK

### MATCHWINNER FOR HIRE

JON STARK
£1000 PER MATCH
PLUS £200 PER GOAL
*No payment for lost game.*

Jon Stark, nicknamed "Superstark" by the fans, was no ordinary player. He was a "freelance" footballer, hiring himself out as a goalscorer to any team that could afford his services. He made his debut in the first issue of SCOOP in 1978, playing a one-off match for 2nd Division Stone Orient, scoring two spectacular goals, against 1st Division Belmoor.

# LIMP-ALONG LESLIE —

Leslie Thomson, king-pin of Darbury Rovers, and ace goal-scorer, played in the pages of WIZARD in the 1950s before his transfer to Hotspur for more success in the '60s.

Nicknamed because of a limp caused by a childhood accident, Leslie was torn between farming and football. The ploughed field on occasions being given priority over the football field.

# THE GOALMAKER. PICKFORD OR PEARSON?

WALTER PEARSON SCORES THE GOAL THAT WON THE LEAGUE CHAMPIONSHIP FOR RIMTHORPE IN 1913

Pickford, or "The Goalmaker" as he came to be known, was football's most mysterious figure. His playing style was similar to other famous footballers of the past — players who had vanished in strange circumstances. Were Pickford, Ted Lucas and Walter Pearson one and the same person?

1948 — First team debut in WIZARD.

1962 — Transferred to VICTOR.

1978 — Mystery man calling himself Capper signs for Redstoke United in the pages of SCOOP.

# IT'S GOALS THAT COUNT! by Nick Smith

This pic shows me with my old pal Arnold Tabbs (left) when we won the Cup while playing for Chidsea F.C. I started my footballing journal in ROVER in the late '40s and continued it in HORNET in 1964. I was transferred to HOTSPUR in 1979 and that's where the above scene appeared.

# CAST, HOOK AND STRIKE!

JOE DODDS lived with his grandfather, Ernie Dodds the haulage contractor. When he wasn't helping on the lorry, Joe was a keen angler.

# CAST, HOOK and STRIKE!

Bernard Briggs was a bloke who got around a bit. Not only did he try every sport you could imagine, but he did it in three different publications — *WIZARD, HOTSPUR* and *HORNET*.

ALL-ROUND BERNARD BRIGGS SPORTSMAN

THE ROVER

ADVENTURE
JUNE 1ST 1940
No. 970
EVERY MONDAY 2ᴰ

SLOGGER DODD

THE HORNET
THE PICTURE-STORY PAPER FOR BOYS
Price 5ᴰ
No. 53—SEPT. 12th, 1964. EVERY TUESDAY.

THE GREATEST BOYS' STORY EVER WRITTEN!

THE TRUTH ABOUT WILSON

IN THIS SELECTION OF GREAT LOOKING SPORTS COVERS...

Heroes came in all shapes and sizes in the great adventure stories. The Hairy Sheriff was a hero, no doubt about that, but he was also an ape! When it came to courage and endurance, the exploits of The Wolf of Kabul made him a household name, but he's best remembered for his faithful servant Chung's choice of weapon . . . a cricket bat! And there was no mightier muscle-man than Morgyn, but his daring deeds and feats of strength were restricted to the African jungle where he could be found wearing only a leopardskin. Three very different heroes with only their courage in common.

# THE HAIRY SHERIFF

# THE HAIRY SHERIFF

THE crackle of gunfire sounded in the main street of the small Western town of Sandstone. It was followed by shouting and a general uproar. A big crowd began to gather outside the bank.

The noise, however, did not disturb Sam Barker, the little ex-circus proprietor, who was now deputy sheriff. Sam, with a stetson over his face, was snoring blissfully at his desk in the sheriff's office.

It was not until the door burst open and a plump, excited figure charged into the office, that Sam blinked his eyes open and sat up. The excited figure was that of Hiram Button, the Mayor of Sandstone.

"Sheriff!" bawled the Mayor. "Where's the sheriff? Why isn't he here? The bank has been robbed," yelled the Mayor. "The bandit got away with a bag of gold dust. He's Red Dawson, a notorious bank robber. It's disgraceful that a thing like this should happen in a law-abiding town. This is what comes," added the Mayor, "of having an ape for a sheriff."

"A human ape," corrected Sam. "Riley, the most intelligent ape in the world."

Riley, the ape, had been the star of Sam's little circus for years. But owing to bad luck Sam had arrived in Sandstone broke, and the show had been sold up. Only Riley was saved.

Luckily, Sam had discovered an old bye-law. Sandstone had been troubled for some years by a bandit and the citizens had decided that whoever could catch the bandit would be given the job of sheriff.

Riley had caught the bandit, with the result that he became sheriff. Sam was his deputy. Riley was quite capable of handling the job, for he was almost

human and could do practically everything except talk properly.

Sam could even understand Riley's "language", and he had always treated the ape as a pal rather than part of his circus.

"Don't you worry about Riley," said Sam to the Mayor. "He'll never let the bank robber get away. I shouldn't be surprised if he isn't bringing him to jail this very minute."

Just then the door opened and a fat, little man trotted in, beaming joyfully. It was Mr Benito, who kept a store down the street.

"The sheriff catcha the bandit!" chirped Mr Benito joyfully. "He catcha him witha da goods on him. He bringa him here right away."

At that moment the Hairy Sheriff marched into the office. Under one brawny arm he held a small, wriggling boy, and under the other a bunch of bananas. Sam and the Mayor blinked at him.

"Where's the bandit?" demanded Sam.

"There he is," explained Mr Benito, pointing to the struggling boy. "He pincha da bananas from my store. The sheriff catcha him plenty quick."

The Mayor uttered a wail of despair.

"Bananas!" he howled. "A bandit robs the bank of hundreds of dollars worth of gold dust, and all the sheriff does is run after a small boy who took a few bananas!"

"I guess Riley always did think bananas were more important than gold dust," sighed Sam. "It's the way he was brought up."

"It's disgraceful!" bawled the Mayor. "The citizens of this town will not put up with it. Unless Red Dawson is caught

and the gold dust recovered, we shall get a new sheriff."

He marched out and slammed the door. Riley, realising that he had not performed his duty to the Mayor's satisfaction, blinked dolefully at Sam. He consoled himself by eating the bananas.

"My bananas!" howled Mr Benito in horror.

"Never mind them," said Sam. "Put it down to working expenses and send the bill to the Mayor. You scram out of here, both of you. Me and the sheriff have got to do a bit of hard thinking."

When the storekeeper and the small boy had gone, Sam frowned at the Hairy Sheriff.

"Listen, Riley, we can't afford to lose our jobs," he said. "You'll have to get after that bandit and bring him back with the gold dust."

"Oke," grunted Riley.

Sam took Riley to the door of the bank that had been robbed. Riley had a nose like a bloodhound and he could follow a trail better than an Indian tracker. It wasn't long before he picked up Red Dawson's trail.

Dawson was heading through the forest towards the hills and the bag of gold dust was tied to his saddle.

The forest gave Riley a big advantage, for the ape was more at home in the trees than on the ground and Dawson had to come off and lead his horse. Dawson was walking along the trail through the forest, when suddenly a hairy leg swung down and gripped his arm. An equally hairy hand came into view with a revolver in it. It was the Hairy Sheriff.

Riley, hanging from the branch of a tree by one hand, held the startled robber dangling in the air. Dawson could hardly believe his senses.

"Leggo!" he screamed. "Great jumping frogs! What is it? Lemme go!"

Riley let him go, and Dawson crashed to the ground. A second later the ape landed on top of him. The bandit had no breath left for fighting after that. The Hairy Sheriff took his gun and tied him up.

Riley felt he had done enough work for one day, so he decided to spend the night in the forest and start back to Sandstone with his prisoner early in the morning. Collecting the bag of gold dust, he left the tied-up bandit on the ground, and looked for a comfortable tree to sleep in.

Riley slept soundly — so soundly that he knew nothing of a strange-looking gentleman in plus-fours and a Panama hat, who came wandering through the forest armed with a torch and a butterfly net.

The strange gent spotted the sleeping sheriff, switched his torch on him and blinked incredulously through thick horn-rimmed glasses.

"Amazing!" burbled the man, shaking with excitement. "Perhaps the Missing Link! Undoubtedly it is some kind of ape man."

Riley suddenly awakened some time later to find himself enmeshed in a strong net of the type that is used to entrap wild animals.

"I shall at once write out a report on the discovery of this ape-man and send it to the Zoological Society. He must be taken at once to New York and put in the zoo," said Professor Bogglewood.

Sam was beginning to get a bit worried about Riley. It was a couple of days since the Hairy Sheriff had set out after Red Dawson. He had not returned and there was no news of him.

"Can't understand it," muttered Sam. "Surely Riley didn't get bumped off by that darned bandit. Riley wouldn't slip up on a simple job like that."

Newspapers from the surrounding towns had just arrived in the sheriff's office. Sam was sitting at his battered desk, glancing idly through them as he pondered over the missing sheriff.

Suddenly a headline caught his eye. It was from the Yellow Creek Herald. It said:

### SENSATIONAL DISCOVERY BY PROFESSOR BOGGLEWOOD.

**Professor Bogglewood and his party, who have been exploring the dense forest land north of Yellow Creek, seeking specimens for his private zoo, have made an amazing discovery. They have definite proof that a strange tribe of ape-men exist in the forest. The Professor has brought one of the apes into Yellow Creek and is to give a lecture on it before sending it away to the zoo. He says the apes must be semi-civilised, for this one had a bag of gold dust in its possession when captured. It also had garments and a sheriff's star, but it is believed that these were stolen from a man who was found tied up nearby.**

"Suffering grapefruit!" yelled Sam, leaping to his feet.

"Sounds like Riley!"

Later, Sam rode into Yellow Creek to find crowds of people making their way towards a hall, outside which was a notice announcing that Professor Bogglewood would lecture on the ape-man that night.

Sam pulled up and stared. Coming along the street was a cart with a cage on it. Inside the cage was the Hairy Sheriff.

"Riley!" yelled Sam, springing off his horse and rushing up to the cage.

"Keep back, my man!" snapped Professor Bogglewood, who was guarding the cage with his colleagues. "Nobody is allowed to touch the exhibit."

"Exhibit my foot! This is no wild man from the woods. This is Riley, the Sheriff of Sandstone City. You let Riley out of that cage," roared Sam, "or I'll — I'll arrest you for kidnapping. I'm the deputy sheriff of Sandstone."

"But this ain't Sandstone," growled a voice. "I'm Sheriff of this town and if there's any arresting to be done I'll do it. What's all the bother?"

Sam explained to the sheriff of Yellow Creek, "You can't put a sheriff in the zoo!" howled Sam. "The law wouldn't allow it."

"The question is," said the sheriff of Yellow Creek, "is the ape human or ain't he human?"

"Well, he's not exactly like you and me," admitted Sam, "but he's got more sense than a lot of guys I know, including the Professor."

"If he ain't human," said the sheriff of Yellow Creek, "he must be an animal. And the law in these parts says that if anybody captures an animal in the forest he's entitled to keep the animal, so I reckon this ape now belongs to the Professor."

Sam scratched his head in despair. If this had been Sandstone City it would have been easy for him to rescue Riley, but he had no authority in Yellow Creek, and it looked as if freeing Riley was going to be a tough job.

At last he made his way to the hall. By that time the Professor had started his lecture. Bogglewood was standing on a rough wooden stage, pointing to a sketch of a primitive man's skull which he had drawn on a blackboard.

Also on the stage was Riley, a chain around his ankle, fastened to a bolt in the floor. Riley was sitting in a chair, and the audience was yelling with laughter, for while Professor Bogglewood was busy at the blackboard, Riley had produced a cigar and was smoking it with great enjoyment.

"Attention, please!" hooted the Professor, coming to the front of the stage and holding up his hand for silence. "This is a serious lecture and I want no unseemly mirth. I want you to study the sketch on the blackboard and notice the shape of the skull, which indicates a very low brain power."

walked out of the saloon, chuckling to himself.

In the meantime the Professor had finished his lecture and taken Riley back in the cage to the hotel where he was staying. Until he could make arrangements to have Riley taken to the zoo, he was keeping the ape in the cage in the hotel yard, guarded by a couple of his assistants.

Riley, however, had no intention of going to a zoo. He was keeping quiet, waiting his opportunity to get free, and that evening the opportunity came.

"I have decided," said the Professor to one of his colleagues, "to take measurements of the ape's cranium, so that I can send a detailed report to the Zoological Society. I shall put a strong sleeping draught in the ape's supper. It will put him into a sound sleep while I make the necessary measurements."

Later that night Riley's supper was brought in. He was about to eat it when a queer, unknown smell hit his sensitive nostrils. He sniffed it again and then emptied it out of the cage. He was a knowing ape and had smelt the sleeping draught. But he was lying flat on his back, snoring loudly, when the Professor came back.

"I thought that sleeping powder would fix him," muttered Professor Bogglewood, and he opened the door of the cage.

But as he bent over Riley, the human ape's legs suddenly shot up and gripped the Professor round the neck. Before the Professor could let out so much as a squeak, Riley had gagged him with his own necktie. Then Riley hopped out of the cage and shut the door, leaving the Professor imprisoned in his place.

The Professor's two assistants saw nothing of this because they were otherwise engaged. The gang of toughs from the saloon had arrived at the gate of the hotel yard and were determined to get in and set Riley free, so that they could follow him to the supposed gold-mine.

"Don't let's argue with these guys," said one of the toughs. "Throw 'em in the horse-trough."

So tossing the two unhappy men in the horse-trough, the toughs marched into the yard and gazed into the cage.

Their jaws dropped in amazement.

"This ain't the ape," yelped one. "It's the Professor. What's happened to the ape?"

"I bet I know," snarled the other. "Remember that little guy who put us up to this idea in the saloon? I bet he set the ape free. He's trying to double-cross us and get that gold-mine for himself."

Sam whistled cheerfully to himself as he waited at the street corner. He knew the toughs had gone to set Riley free. He had watched them. Now he was waiting, expecting to see his hairy pal come ambling down the street at any moment.

But it was not Riley; it was the toughs who came down the street. One of them spotted Sam, and he was quickly surrounded by an angry mob.

"You'd better talk fast, wise guy!" snapped the leader. "That ape wasn't in the cage. You must have let him out. Where is he?"

"I don't know," gasped Sam.

"Quit stalling!" roared the tough. "No guy is going to double-cross us over

---

The audience, to the amazement and indignation of the Professor, gave way to another burst of mirth. Riley, when the Professor's back was turned, had rubbed the sketch out and chalked a rough picture of the Professor himself in its place!

"Cut out the funny stuff, Riley," hooted Sam. "How, for Pete's sake, did you let this Professor guy sneak up on you and put you in irons?"

"Uh?" Riley spotted Sam and began jibbering away excitedly.

He was explaining to Sam what had happened in the forest, but Professor Bogglewood thought he was working himself into a state of dangerous rage.

"Throw that man out of here," he yelled, pointing to Sam. "He's trying to cause a disturbance. He's upsetting the ape and ruining my lecture."

A couple of burly attendants grasped the protesting Sam and slung him out of the hall.

Riley growled. He had been anxious to tell Sam something else. Sitting unnoticed at the back of the hall was a red-haired, scowling fellow. It was Red Dawson, the bandit.

The unsuspecting Professor had released Red when he found him tied up in the forest, but Red hadn't got his bag of gold dust back. He had been trailing the Professor ever since, waiting for a chance to get it.

"I've got to do something," groaned Sam, "I can't let poor old Riley finish up his days in the zoo."

He thought hard for a time and suddenly an idea came to him. Half a dozen toughs were playing cards in the nearby saloon.

"I'd sure like to find out where that gold-mine is," said Sam loudly. "It ought to be worth a fortune to the guy who locates it."

"What gold-mine?" said one of the toughs.

"There must be a gold-mine somewhere," said Sam. "Didn't that ape have a bag of gold dust on him when old Bogglewood captured him? The ape must know where the gold is. Suppose the ape was set free. Sooner or later he'd go back to the gold-mine. All a guy would have to do is to follow him."

The toughs exchanged glances. It was clear that the idea appealed to them. Sam

# THE HAIRY SHERIFF

that gold-mine. You ain't aiming to be strung up to the nearest tree, are you?"

"I — I was kidding," gulped Sam. "There isn't any gold-mine. It — it was just a joke. The Professor didn't find any bag of gold dust on the ape. That — that was just a newspaper publicity stunt —"

"How dare you tell such an untruth, sir!" bawled an infuriated voice.

The Professor came charging up. He had been let out of the cage by one of his assistants. He held a heavy bag in his hands.

"There was a bag of gold dust," he roared. "Here it is! I've just been to my room to get it. I am going to give it to the man who recaptures that ape for me."

"You can't do that," spluttered Sam. "That's stolen property. I'll have the law on you —"

"You are the one who will be dealt with by the law," declared Professor Bogglewood. "I am convinced that you had a hand in the escape of that ape. A few days in jail will do you good. Help me get him along to the sheriff's office, men, and then we'll go after the ape."

Struggling furiously, Sam was marched down the street by the Professor and the toughs. Before they got to the jail, however, a strange thing happened. A hairy face suddenly appeared round a corner.

"It's the ape!" yelled the Professor. "Get after him, you fools. The gold dust goes to the one who catches him."

They all charged after Riley, leaving Sam alone. Riley dodged his pursuers with ease, circled a block of buildings and came back to the spot where Sam was standing.

"Good work, pal," grinned Sam. "But we've got to get out of here before that crazy Professor comes back. If he catches us again we're sunk."

Riley grunted and started off down the street. He still had a job to do and he wasn't going back to Sandstone until he had done it. The little matter of Red Dawson and the gold dust was on his mind.

In the meantime Red was busy. He was still keeping a close watch on the Professor and his helpers who were searching the town for the runaway ape. Red approached the Professor. "Listen, Professor, I can lead you to the ape. But get rid of these other guys first. The ape might get scared off if a crowd goes after him."

The Professor told the toughs to search one end of the town while he searched the other. Then, with some rope to bind the ape when he was caught, the Professor set off with Red Dawson. They left the town and took the trail that led to the forest. They tramped on until the Professor began to get tired. "Are you sure the ape went this way?"

"I don't know where the ape went and I don't care," grinned Red Dawson. "What I'm after is that bag of gold dust. Hand it over."

"What!" Professor Bogglewood blinked. "Certainly not! You'll get the gold when I get the ape."

"I'll have the gold now!" Dawson, to the Professor's horror, produced a gun.

The Professor handed over the bag. Just at that moment a hairy shape dropped out of the tree. It landed on top of the bandit and flattened him to the ground. It was the Hairy Sheriff.

"My ape!" gasped the Professor.

"Your nothing," said Sam Barker, coming out from behind the trees. "We've been trailing you all the way from Yellow Creek. We waited until we got into the Sandstone district in order to make things legal. This is Riley's territory, and he's Sheriff, and any guy who tries to interfere with him is going to end up in the jug. Ain't that so, Riley?"

"Uh-uh!" grinned the Hairy Sheriff.

But after being held up by a bandit, Professor Bogglewood was in no mood to interfere again. He went sadly back to Yellow Creek, and Sam and Riley returned to Sandstone with the gold dust and their prisoner.

DESIGNED BY A SWEDISH ENGINEER, THIS PLANE IS A COMBINATION OF SEAPLANE, AUTOGYRO AND HELICOPTER!

This American is so scared of being lost that he has his name tattooed on his legs in dozens of different languages.

A SIX-ROUND BOXING MATCH BETWEEN TWO ROBOTS WAS RECENTLY HELD IN CALIFORNIA! IN THE HEAT OF BATTLE, BOTH OF THEM WENT ON FIRE, AND FELL TO THE GROUND IN FLAMES.

Two bald Americans held a hair growing championship for a purse of 50 dollars!

# Strange BUT TRUE! PART II

More facts, figures and fun from the files of ADVENTURE

The shrew is so slim that it will pass through a finger ring—yet it eats 24 meals a day!

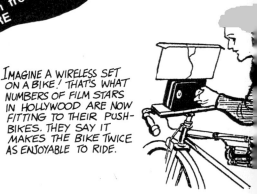

BICYCLE STAND ATTACHED TO PEDAL →

THIS GERMAN INVENTION MAKES CYCLING IN HEAVY TRAFFIC MUCH EASIER AND SAFER. IF THE RIDER HAS TO STOP SUDDENLY, THEN HE SIMPLY PRESSES THE RELEASE ON THE PEDAL AND THE STAND FALLS INTO PLACE.

Cure for sea-sickness by an old Berkshire woman—"As you walk up the gangway, swallow a live spider."

A SIMPLE MACHINE, BUT CLEVER ALL THE SAME — THIS BREAD-KNIFE CUTS SLICES OF EQUAL THICKNESS ALL THE TIME.

IMAGINE A WIRELESS SET ON A BIKE! THAT'S WHAT NUMBERS OF FILM STARS IN HOLLYWOOD ARE NOW FITTING TO THEIR PUSH-BIKES. THEY SAY IT MAKES THE BIKE TWICE AS ENJOYABLE TO RIDE.

TO INDICATE TO FOLLOWING CARS THAT IT IS CHANGING DIRECTION, THIS REAR SIGNAL PROJECTS LIGHTED WORDS ON TO THE ROAD. THERE CAN BE NO MISTAKE ABOUT THIS WORDING.

WHILE RUSHING THROUGH THE AIR AT 100 M.P.H. THIS AIRMAN CATCHES GERMS IN THE TRAP WHICH HE HOLDS IN HIS HANDS. ALL HE DOES IS TO CLOSE THE TWO PARTS TOGETHER!

BY MEANS OF THIS SIMPLE DEVICE, CALLED THE VOCALPHONE, A SINGER MAY HEAR HIS OWN VOICE EXACTLY AS IT SOUNDS TO THE AUDIENCE. THE VOCALPHONE RETURNS THE VOICE TO THE SINGER'S EAR.

TURNING

# MORGYN the MIGHTY

MORGYN THE MIGHTY was seated in the hut of Ndalo, Chief of the Bawalo tribe, eating a hearty meal. Opposite him sat Ndalo, and several other members of the tribe, waiting patiently till Morgyn finished his meal.

Morgyn's arrival in this village had come about in a strange way. Earlier that day, he had fallen into a pit dug by the Bawalos to protect their village from intruders. The Bawalos, finding Morgyn there, had been about to kill him at first, but on learning that Morgyn had come from the nearby plateau which they believed to be inhabited by evil spirits, they had invited him to their village to help them against a strange enemy.

"In what way can I be of help?" demanded Morgyn the Mighty, as he finished his meal.

Ndalo, Chief of the Bawalo tribe, trembled as he explained.

"My warriors are brave, as brave as any in Africa, but they cannot deal with spirits. Only you, who have come through the Country of the Clouds without harm could deal with Mongoa for us."

"But what is Mongoa? What is it like?" asked Morgyn.

Again the Chief shivered. The mere mention of Mongoa seemed to send him into a panic. The men who had come into the hut with him now sat silently around the foot of the walls, listening and holding their heads.

Ndalo went on to explain that Mongoa had appeared about two years before, one dark night when there was no moon. Beyond the fields at the back of the village there was a great swamp, and one night there had come a sudden foul smell on the wind from that direction, as though the mud in the swamp had been stirred up.

The smell had become stronger, and the natives had heard the sound of heavy, dragging feet outside their stockade, which at that time was made of thorn. The mysterious sounds had struck fear into the villagers' hearts. They had rushed into their huts and had shut themselves in.

A little later there had been crashing noises, as though something of great size was forcing its way through the thick, thorn stockade, and they knew that the evil intruder was within their village. No one had dared look, no one had dared make a sound.

The intruder had prowled about for some time, then had come the crash of a falling hut, the shrieks of the family who had lived in it, and loud, crunching noises. After that the villagers had heard the monster go out through the stockade and return to the swamp.

All that night they had cowered in their huts, but in the morning they had gone out with the daylight, and had discovered that the hut of Kongwa, the son of Kosaki, had been knocked down, and that all its occupants had vanished.

"Did you not find out what the monster was like?" demanded Morgyn.

"Not then, not for many weeks afterwards, for we were too terrified to look at first," explained Ndalo. "The ju-ju man said it was an evil spirit, and that it would go away when it had taken toll of us, but that if we looked at it we would all die. We believed him, until one night he was taken and eaten, then we knew that he understood no more about it than the rest of us. Some of us waited for Mongoa the following night and when it broke through the stockade as though it was made of grass we saw —"

His eyes bulged, and he licked his lips as if afraid to continue.

"Yes?" snapped Morgyn. "You saw what?"

"Mongoa was like a crocodile, but larger than any that really exist," went on the chief. "It was as tall as a man and as long as the biggest war canoe. Its tail curved over and moved in the air like a snake rearing up. Its eyes were blazing with fire, smoke came from its nostrils, and its mouth could have swallowed a whole bullock. That is what we saw."

"What happened after that?" Morgyn asked.

"We hid ourselves, and the next day set to work to build the great wall which now surrounds our village," the Chief continued. "Night after night Mongoa came and destroyed part of our work, but we persevered, and now the village is safe."

"Mongoa cannot get inside the wall now?" queried Morgyn.

"No, but it prowls about outside, and makes the night hideous with its cries," answered the Chief. "Sometimes Mongoa blazes with fire, and shines in the dark. That is how we know that it is a spirit."

"Blazes with fire!" exclaimed Morgyn in disbelief. "I would like to see this monster of yours."

Just then a drum began to rumble somewhere in the village. It was a big drum, and someone was banging it lustily. The men in the hut leapt to their feet. Their eyes showed their terror.

"Mongoa has appeared! That is the signal. We have watchers on the walls," said the Chief.

Morgyn joined the others in the doorway.

"I would like to see the monster," he said, and took up his club.

Ndalo shouted to someone in the darkness, outside, and got a reply.

"Mongoa is outside the main gate," he said, turning to Morgyn. "You shall have your wish."

Morgyn accompanied the villagers to the gate. A ladder at one side of the gate led to a closed platform which stuck out above the gate, and two trembling guards crouched on this, pointing silently downwards. Morgyn became aware of an evil smell, the sort of smell that comes to the surface when black mud is stirred up at the bottom of a stagnant pool. Morgyn climbed up to the platform and knelt down.

The men would not look themselves, but again pointed. Morgyn lay at full length on the floor of the platform, and peered through an opening there. Then his hands clenched, and every muscle in his great body became rigid and tense. Just below him he saw an amazing sight.

The villagers had not lied when they had declared that Mongoa shone in the dark. The monster outside the gate glowed with a ghostly light, not brightly, but sufficiently to reveal its hideous shape.

The creature must have been forty feet long, not counting the tail, which curved up over its back like the tail of a scorpion. As he studied it Morgyn saw that it was a giant crocodile, and its head was gnarled and knotted with age. It had a long snout, and evil eyes above it. Its mouth was shut as it nosed and prodded at one of the spears sticking out from the gate, but as Morgyn watched, the monster suddenly made a quick snap, and the spear broke off, bitten in half by those huge jaws and wicked teeth.

"It is a giant crocodile," Morgyn announced to the villagers.

There were murmurs of disagreement from the natives behind him. Morgyn picked up one of the heavy spears which stood around the covered platform, pushed the pointed end through one of the openings in the floor, and drove the weapon downwards with all his might.

The spear struck with a thud in the centre of the monster's back and bounced off again. A snort came from it, and it raised its head, opening its mighty jaws.

The monster's tail suddenly swung round and up, and struck the thick planking on which Morgyn crouched, splintering it and jarring him violently.

Morgyn chose another spear, and sent it hurtling downwards.

This time the spear went inside the brute's mouth, and the monster's jaws slammed shut as the point struck its tongue. A deep roaring sound came from somewhere within the monster's throat, and it lashed its tail from side to side.

For more than five minutes it beat at the gate and the wall with its massive tail, smashing spears and chipping the hard mud. Mad with rage it was trying to get at the men who were inside but the defences proved too strong. Eventually it turned and went away towards the swamp and the last Morgyn saw of it was the glow which outlined it in the darkness.

He came down and told the villagers that their "evil spirit" was a giant crocodile of extreme age.

Ndalo shook his head stubbornly.

"It is no crocodile. My men are not afraid of crocodiles, but we are afraid of Mongoa. It is a demon from the swamp."

"Very well," agreed Morgyn, seeing it was useless to argue. "Tomorrow I will make preparations to kill your demon."

Even in daylight the villagers were not keen to go near the swamp, but Morgyn followed the tracks of the monster across the fields and right down to the edge of the vast area of slime and ooze that stretched as far as the eye could see. The only things that grew in the swamp were fantastically-shaped mangrove trees, festooned with unhealthy-looking creepers.

Judging by the path worn across the fields the crocodile always came out of the swamp at the same spot, and took more or less the same route to the village every night. Morgyn stared at the swamp, and wondered where the brute slept by day. Probably it was in one of the clumps of mangroves.

Morgyn returned to the grove of bamboos growing just outside the village, and some of the villagers watched in awe as he exerted his strength to break off a long branch of bamboo about five inches in diameter. He had borrowed one of the local men's home-made axes, and with this he cut a length of about five feet sharply pointing it at either end. The points he hardened in a fire, then took the tough, thick rod in his hands and slowly bent it until the points met.

Grunts of admiration came from his watchers. No two men amongst them could have doubled the bamboo like that.

"A pig must be killed — a good fat pig," Morgyn ordered.

A pig was chosen and killed as Morgyn had ordered. Morgyn carried the carcass halfway to the swamp, and there placed it on the ground behind some bushes. Again he doubled the powerful bamboo rod, and forced both ends together into the broadest part of the pig. That had the effect of keeping the bamboo bent, with the points close together and he went on pushing the U-shaped bamboo further and further into the flesh until it was almost invisible.

The villagers began to understand what he was planning and shook their heads.

"Mongoa will not be caught like that," they said. "It will know that is a trap before it touches the pig."

Morgyn said nothing. He asked for ropes and plaited three of these together to form a strong hawser. He made a noose in one end of this, and tied the other end to a tree close to the place where the gigantic crocodile was in the habit of coming out of the swamp.

Morgyn had one more task to carry out. This was to cut down a stout sapling and to fashion himself a spear some fifteen feet long. The point of this he also hardened with fire. These preparations finished, Morgyn settled down to rest till nightfall for Mongoa never appeared till then.

When it was almost dark Morgyn picked up the dead pig and carried it down to the edge of the swamp, where he placed it near the solitary tree. He then climbed into the tree, taking with him the noosed end of the plaited rope, his club and the new spear which he had made.

The evening drew on, and the first pale stars came out. The wind changed direction, and Morgyn was aware of an evil smell, the smell of stirred-up mud.

Then he heard the slapping of mud as it was displaced by a powerful swimmer. The giant crocodile was coming and it was half in and half on top of the mud.

Finally it reached the edge of the swamp, and reared itself slowly on to firm ground flicking its tail from side to side and high over its back. Mud flew in all directions. The mass of slimy vegetation on its back quickly dried and showed white in the darkness. A faint glow came from the layer of mud that continually coated the monster. Morgyn guessed that there was a good deal of phosphorus in the swamp and that was the reason for the ghostly light that came from the beast.

The crocodile was in no hurry. When it climbed to the top of the bank it slowly turned its head from side to side, as though sniffing the air. While doing this it scented the dead pig no more than twenty yards away, and at once turned in that direction.

Morgyn knew his time was coming, and tensed. The pig lay on its side, the embedded bent bamboo hidden. The crocodile lowered its hideous head and sniffed the bait. Morgyn saw the monster's great jaws suddenly open, and the next moment the entire pig was engulfed.

The monster raised its head as it began to chew, and seemed to be staring straight at the tree when the trap was sprung. The movement of its jaws disturbed the bent bamboo stake and it was dislodged from the meat.

Springing out with great violence one pointed end of the bamboo stake was buried in the roof of the monster's mouth and the other end pierced its tongue. So startling and unexpected was this that the great brute reared up on its hindlegs, roaring with rage and pain. Then it began to turn, twist, and roll on the ground doing everything it could to get rid of the painful object in its mouth.

Morgyn waited with the noosed rope in his hand leaning down from the branch as he did so. When his chance came he dropped the noose over the end of the threshing tail, and jerked it tight.

In its agony the monster now decided to make back for the swamp. As it moved away from the tree the rope became taut, and the tail, which had been previously curved over its back, was pulled out straight behind it.

The crocodile became aware of something holding it at the rear and it whirled around with a speed that was extraordinary in a creature of that size.

Round and round the tree it plunged. The rope shortened as the monster circled, and it was drawn in close to the tree. Morgyn had not expected this, and watched grimly as the crocodile tried to snap at the foot of the tree. Each time it attempted to close its jaws the spiked ends of the bamboo stake drove deeper, and the pain caused it to stop. Morgyn decided that it was time to use his spear.

Bracing himself with his back to the trunk and his legs astride one of the branches of the tree, Morgyn reached down and stabbed for one of the monster's glaring eyes. He missed by an inch, and the point of the spear slipped as though on steel. He almost overbalanced.

Ineffective though the stab had been, the monster became even angrier, drew back a few yards, and again charged the tree, at the same time rearing up to its full height.

The tree swayed and quivered. The brute must have weighed two tons, and the force of its attack nearly uprooted

Morgyn's refuge. He had to cling on with both hands to prevent himself from falling.

He gritted his teeth, and tightened his grasp on the spear. He had made up his mind to free the villagers of this menace, and he meant to see it through. If he could not drive the spear home he would get closer. He still had his knife!

He made one more attempt with the spear. This time it slipped off the monster's scaly hide and buried its point in the ground. Morgyn let go of the spear, drew his knife, and dropped from his perch astride the gnarled neck of the giant crocodile.

Morgyn landed just behind the crocodile's head and clung on to steady himself. The monster did not feel Morgyn's arrival. It went on butting at the tree and trying to snap with its wicked teeth, always driving the points of the stake deeper into its flesh.

It had now started to circle the other way which meant the rope was unwinding. Morgyn, on the monster's back, gripped tightly with his knees, and leaned well forward. It was his intention to stab the crocodile in the jaw.

Morgyn worked himself into position, grasped one of the gnarled bumps that stuck out from the top of the monster's head to steady himself and drove his knife to the hilt into the monster's gaping mouth.

The stricken crocodile leapt up in the air, rearing on its hind legs so suddenly that Morgyn was almost thrown from its back. At first he clung with knees and one hand, then was forced to throw both his arms about the monster's thick neck and cling on for dear life.

Coming down on all fours, the half-crazed crocodile darted away to the left. The rope tightened, there was a creaking sound, the snapping of roots underground, and to Morgyn's horror the tree to which the crocodile was tied began to topple over. With a rush the sixty-foot tree crashed to the ground.

Morgyn the Mighty winced, for he expected to be pinned beneath the falling tree, but the crocodile darted to the full length of the rope and only its tail was held by the weight of the tree.

The crocodile began another mad struggle to free its tail and while it was going on, Morgyn the Mighty took the opportunity to reach forward and drive his knife once more into the monster's unprotected mouth.

This time he was ready for the wild outburst that would follow his stab. He had hoped to weaken the crocodile severely with his knife-thrusts, but realised he had failed. His attacks had merely angered the giant crocodile and it seemed as strong as ever. With a supreme effort, it pulled its tail from underneath the tree, and made off for the swamp, towing that great tree behind it.

The great beast, incensed by Morgyn's attacks, jerked its head from side to side, its eyes ablaze. The tree, with its wide spreading branches, offered great opposition to being pulled along.

Twice it turned over, and Morgyn saw that to remain where he was would be madness. He now had not only to avoid the lashing tail of the crocodile, but also the swirling branches of the tree. He waited his chance and leapt into the darkness, landing lightly on hands and

knees. The next moment he was up and darting away to one side.

With heaving chest and legs apart, Morgyn the Mighty watched the crocodile dive into the mud at the edge of the swamp. The tree got stuck on the edge, and went no farther. There was the sound of splashing, of gurgling and sucking as the crocodile plunged first this way and then another. The plaited ropes would not snap, and the noose would not slip. The crocodile was anchored fast by its tail to the shore. Tug as it did, it could not get free.

Morgyn swiftly went back to the place where the spear stood upright in the ground, and tugged it free. Running lightly, he gained the bank above the place where the tethered monster struggled to free itself.

Morgyn's knife had only served to irritate the crocodile, as pin-pricks might irritate a man — perhaps the spear would do better.

He waited his chance, straining his eyes in the gloom, until the moment came when his hand moved with the speed of sight itself, and he sent the hardened point of his spear far down into one of the wounds which his knife had previously made.

The crocodile gave a great shudder, plunging so deeply into the mud that Morgyn was forced to release his hold on the spear. The tail swished close to his head, then dropped limply on the bank. The monster did not move again. The victory had been hard fought, but it was Morgyn's. He had succeeded in killing Mongoa!

Morgyn stepped back and watched the bubbles bursting and the stirred mud settling. The rope still held to the tree, preventing the monster from sinking out of sight in the mud, and Morgyn was glad of this, for now he could show Ndalo and the others that he had rid them of the "evil spirit" which had made their life a misery for so long.

When he had recovered his breath he turned and ran back to the gate of the village. It was quite dark, for low clouds now obscured the sky, but he could hear the murmur of voices beyond the wall. Nobody in the village had slept that night. They had been listening to the terrible sounds outside.

"Hullo there!" Morgyn shouted in the local dialect. "It is done! Mongoa is dead. You can open your gates. Mongoa is no more. I have slain it!"

Inside the village there was silence at first as if the villagers could not believe their ears. Then as the meaning of Morgyn's words dawned on them, there were cheers and wild outbursts of joy. The gates were flung open, and Morgyn was given a terrific welcome.

Bonfires were lit, and the natives danced around them. It looked like being the greatest festival the tribe had ever known.

But when the noise was at its height, Morgyn crept away from the others and into the Chief's hut. Nobody was there, for all were making merry outside. He flung himself down on the piled lion skins, and went to sleep.

The celebrations were still continuing when he wakened to find the sun already high. When Morgyn appeared in the doorway of the hut the villagers rushed to hoist him onto a shield.

Out through the great gateway they carried him, down to the edge of the swamp, where nothing could be seen of the giant crocodile but the end of its tail and the thick hawser holding it to the tree. Morgyn went forward and grasped the plaited rope.

I need ten strong men to help me," he called. "There is no danger. Who are the strongest men in the tribe?"

There was a rush to claim the honour, and he placed them five on either side of the rope, took the place of honour at the end himself, and gave the signal for the others to heave.

It needed a long pull and a strong pull. Morgyn pulled with the strength of six, and it was chiefly by his efforts that the hideous monster, caked with mud, was finally hauled on to the bank.

A great cry went up from the villagers as they crowded round their terrible foe. Here was the monster which had plagued their nights for two years, the brute which had devoured so many of their relatives and friends. They swarmed over it, stamping and stabbing with their spears. They called it names, they heaped insults upon it, and in the midst of all this noise and confusion, the man who had made it possible for them to be free of fear, turned away and slipped off into the jungle to continue his journey home.

**Morgyn's mighty adventures originally appeared in ROVER, and then, from the 1960s onwards, as picture stories in VICTOR.**

# Adventure

"Fetch the Black Stone from the Burial Place of the Elephants" — that was the test set for Morgyn the Mighty by Bendugu, chief priest of the temple of Goz. The world's strongest man had become the champion of King Wassulu of the Koroko tribe in a bid to undergo successfully, terrible tests, thus breaking the evil power of Bendugu and his priests. Now with Ubangi, the king's son, Morgyn was spying on an elephant herd.

LOOKS AS IF OUR WEARY DAYS OF WATCHING THIS HERD ARE ENDED, UBANGI. THAT OLD TUSKER IS BEING HELPED ON HIS LAST JOURNEY TO THE BURIAL PLACE OF THE ELEPHANTS.

WE MUST BE VERY CAREFUL, O CHAMPION. IF THE YOUNG ELEPHANTS SCENT US THEY WILL HUNT US DOWN AND KILL US TO KEEP THE BURIAL PLACE SECRET.

THE BURIAL PLACE MUST BE SOMEWHERE AMONGST THAT RANGE OF HILLS.

THE SWAMP OF TENEBRA LIES BETWEEN THE HILLS AND THE ELEPHANTS. THE SWAMP IS BOTTOMLESS AND NO ANIMALS OR HUMANS CAN CROSS IT.

I CAN'T BELIEVE MY EYES. WHY ARE THE ELEPHANTS NOT SINKING INTO THE SWAMP? IS IT MAGIC?

THERE MUST BE A FIRM CAUSEWAY UNDER THE TOP LAYER OF MUD AND THE ELEPHANTS CAN INSTINCTIVELY FOLLOW IT. QUICK, LAD, WE MUST COLLECT SOME LONG, STRAIGHT STICKS.

PUT A STICK IN WHENEVER THE HIDDEN CAUSEWAY CHANGES DIRECTION. I CAN FAINTLY SEE THE TRACK LEFT BY THE ELEPHANTS. YOU CAN WORK ON MY TRACKS.

I UNDERSTAND, O CHAMPION.

I HAVE BUT TWO STICKS LEFT, O CHAMPION.

THAT WILL BE ENOUGH. THE CAUSEWAY GOES STRAIGHT FROM HERE TO THE MOUTH OF THAT CLEFT THE ELEPHANTS ARE NOW ENTERING.

WHAT ARE THEY DOING?

MY GUESS IS THAT THEY'RE TRYING TO UNCOVER A HIDDEN TUNNEL.

YOU WERE RIGHT, O CHAMPION. NOW WHAT DO WE DO?

WAIT A WHILE, THEN FOLLOW THE ELEPHANTS.

# MORGYN THE MIGHTY

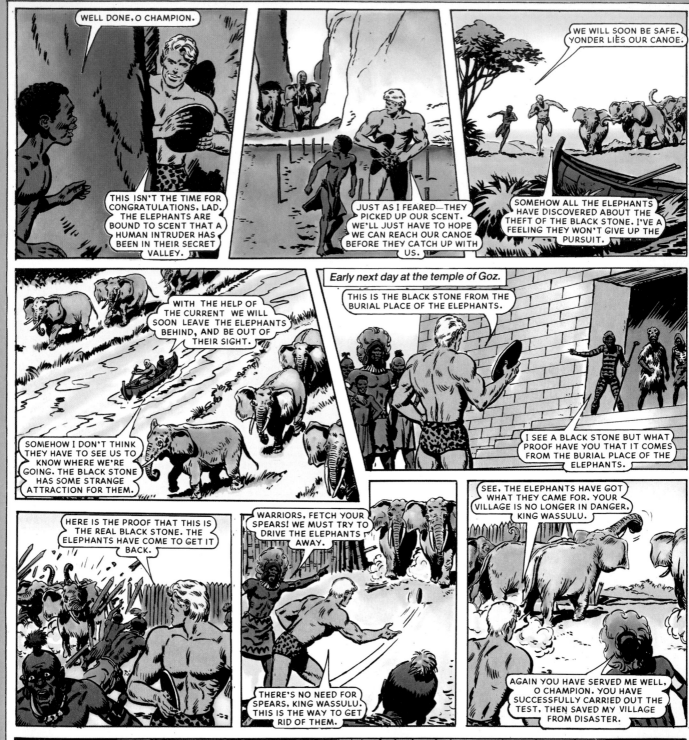

WELL DONE, O CHAMPION.

THIS ISN'T THE TIME FOR CONGRATULATIONS, LAD. THE ELEPHANTS ARE BOUND TO SCENT THAT A HUMAN INTRUDER HAS BEEN IN THEIR SECRET VALLEY.

JUST AS I FEARED—THEY PICKED UP OUR SCENT. WE'LL JUST HAVE TO HOPE WE CAN REACH OUR CANOE BEFORE THEY CATCH UP WITH US.

WE WILL SOON BE SAFE. YONDER LIES OUR CANOE.

SOMEHOW ALL THE ELEPHANTS HAVE DISCOVERED ABOUT THE THEFT OF THE BLACK STONE. I'VE A FEELING THEY WON'T GIVE UP THE PURSUIT.

WITH THE HELP OF THE CURRENT WE WILL SOON LEAVE THE ELEPHANTS BEHIND, AND BE OUT OF THEIR SIGHT.

SOMEHOW I DON'T THINK THEY HAVE TO SEE US TO KNOW WHERE WE'RE GOING. THE BLACK STONE HAS SOME STRANGE ATTRACTION FOR THEM.

*Early next day at the temple of Goz.*

THIS IS THE BLACK STONE FROM THE BURIAL PLACE OF THE ELEPHANTS.

I SEE A BLACK STONE BUT WHAT PROOF HAVE YOU THAT IT COMES FROM THE BURIAL PLACE OF THE ELEPHANTS.

HERE IS THE PROOF THAT THIS IS THE REAL BLACK STONE. THE ELEPHANTS HAVE COME TO GET IT BACK.

WARRIORS, FETCH YOUR SPEARS! WE MUST TRY TO DRIVE THE ELEPHANTS AWAY.

THERE'S NO NEED FOR SPEARS, KING WASSULU. THIS IS THE WAY TO GET RID OF THEM.

SEE, THE ELEPHANTS HAVE GOT WHAT THEY CAME FOR. YOUR VILLAGE IS NO LONGER IN DANGER, KING WASSULU.

AGAIN YOU HAVE SERVED ME WELL, O CHAMPION. YOU HAVE SUCCESSFULLY CARRIED OUT THE TEST, THEN SAVED MY VILLAGE FROM DISASTER.

AGAIN HE HAS TRIUMPHED, BENDUGU. IF HE SUCCEEDS IN THE NEXT TEST OUR POWER WILL BE DESTROYED FOREVER.

THAT, I WILL NOT ALLOW TO HAPPEN, FULALA. I WILL MAKE SURE THE TEST IS ONE THAT WILL BE IMPOSSIBLE FOR EVEN A MAN AS STRONG AS HE IS.

*Several hours later.*

GOZ HAS TOLD ME WHAT THE FINAL TEST IS TO BE, O CHAMPION. YOU HAVE ONE HOUR FROM NOON TOMORROW TO STOP THIS WIND BLOWING ON THE TEMPLE.

GOZ HAS SET YOU AN IMPOSSIBLE TASK. EVEN YOUR AMAZING STRENGTH IS NOT EQUAL TO BUILDING A GIANT FENCE AROUND THE TEMPLE IN SO SHORT A TIME.

BENDUGU HAS THOUGHT UP A CUNNING SCHEME BUT I THINK THERE IS ONE WAY I CAN SUCCEED BY USING MY BRAINS AS WELL AS MY BRAWN, KING WASSULU.

*Later accompanied by Ubangi, Morgyn was hard at work.*

WHY HAVE YOU CUT DOWN THAT PALM TREE, O CHAMPION?

BECAUSE IT'S THE SPRINGIEST TREE IN THE JUNGLE. I'M GOING TO USE IT TO GIVE BENDUGU A NASTY SHOCK.

YOU CAN HELP ME, UBANGI, BY CUTTING LONG LENGTHS OF THE STRONGEST LIANA YOU CAN FIND. ONCE I'VE TRIMMED THIS TREE I HAVE MORE TREE-FELLING TO DO.

*Shortly before dusk.*

THAT'S ENOUGH LIANA, LAD. ONCE I'VE FINISHED WITH THIS BRANCH EVERYTHING IS READY. WE CAN DO NOTHING MORE UNTIL THE VILLAGE IS ASLEEP.

NEXT, WE'VE GOT TO GET THIS LOT UP TO THE TEMPLE ROOF AS QUIETLY AS POSSIBLE. I'LL CLIMB UP, LOWER ONE END OF THE LIANA AND YOU TIE THE LOGS ON, LAD.

I UNDERSTAND, O CHAMPION.

THIS PLAN OF MINE SEEMS CRAZY, BUT IT'S THE ONLY WAY I CAN THINK OF TRYING TO OUTWIT BENDUGU.

COVER STORY

WIZARD

INTO ACTION WITH
"THE WOLF OF KABUL",
CHUNG AND "CLICKY-BA."

ADVENTURE

STRANG THE TERRIBLE
IS BACK AGAIN

13TH 1940

EVERY MONDAY

# THE GREAT ADVENTURES

WHEN THE GREAT ADVENTURE STORIES WERE ORIGINALLY PUBLISHED, THEY APPEARED IN BLACK AND WHITE. BUT FANS OF THE WOLF OF KABUL AND STRANG THE TERRIBLE DID HAVE ONE CHANCE EVERY WEEK TO SEE THEIR HEROES IN COLOUR, ON BOLD BRIGHT ACTION-PACKED COVERS LIKE THESE.

THE SKIPPER
No 513 — JUNE 29TH 1940 — PRICE 2D

WHERE IS THE BOY?

THE ROVER
No 968 NOV. 2ND 1940 EVERY THURSDAY 2D

ADVENTURE
INSIDE A WESTERN THRILLER
The THIRTEENTH TRIP OF THE DEADWOOD COACH

# The Laughing Pirate

## A swashbuckling tale from ROVER

THE long line of moving objects in the swamp scarcely resembled human beings, so bent, so plastered with mud, and so heavily laden were they. Yet they were men, Englishmen, and triumphant.

On their backs they bore gold to the value of many thousands of pounds, gold which they had taken from the Spanish mule-train which crossed Panama twice each season. They had taken the Dons unawares, thirty miles inland, when they had been quite unprepared for attack, and this was the result. That treasure which should have been shipped from Santa Isabel to Spain, was going to be loaded on to the stout brig St. George.

Splashing up and down the line of exhausted men, lending a hand here, easing a load there, encouraging with word and joke, was Sir Daniel Darnby, the Laughing Pirate, who had made the attack possible.

"Step out, me merry lads!" he roared, his eyes flashing above his mask of mud. "The creek's no more than a mile ahead. We're nearly there, lads. Step out! Once we're at sea all the Dons on the Spanish Main won't lay us by the heels. We'll head for home — and fortune!"

His words inspired them. Tired eyes glittered with hope. Men forgot the leeches, the mosquitoes, and the eternal mud which clogged their feet and rose to their knees.

In the rear, hurrying along all stragglers, supporting those who slipped, was Bill Bullock, the mate of the St. George. He had been with the Laughing Pirate on many an adventure, but none more to his liking than this.

Twenty minutes later Sir Daniel waved his sword in the air, and yelled:

"I see her masts! The St. George! We're nearly there, me hearties. They've not failed us. Ben Rogers has kept his tryst."

More than one of that reckless party gulped with relief when they saw the tapering masts and the sleek lines of the St. George out in the centre of the creek. This was the moment for which they had longed. When they had gone ashore to snatch the ill-gotten Spanish gold from its late owners, they had left a skeleton crew of six men and the bo'sun aboard, with instructions to remain at anchor, hidden from the sea in this remote creek.

"Ahoy, there!" roared the Laughing Pirate, in a voice which roused the echoes and sent the parrots fluttering from the swamp trees. "Send the boats ashore, me lads! We're back and heavily laden. We've pickings for all, an' —"

"The boats are already on the beach, Sir Daniel," pointed out someone. "Rogers expects us. I can see someone waving from the poop-deck."

"Then the sooner we're aboard, and out of this stinking mud, the better," chuckled Sir Daniel, tossing back his head with a characteristic gesture. "Divide into two parties, me hearties."

Somehow they found strength to reach the boats, to dump their heavy loads aboard, to wash their mired legs in the cool, salt water, and to get the craft afloat. One and all piled aboard with grunts of thankfulness. The past was like a nightmare which fades away at the coming of daylight.

There was a light breeze which whipped the spume from their oars. Their fatigue was forgotten as they bumped alongside the St. George. It was like coming home. To them she was a piece of England. Sight of the flag brought lumps to their throats. Men snatched at ropes and made fast.

Swifter than any of them was Sir Daniel Darnby. Without waiting for a ladder to be lowered, he swarmed up a rope and gained the deck with an agile leap which gave the lie to his weariness.

"Ahoah, there, Rogers! Williams! Sutcliffe! Horn! Where are ye? Why hide yourselves at a time like this? Break out the grog, me lads!"

The flag flapped weakly, but there was no other sound as the muddy, bleary-eyed men hauled themselves aboard, hoisting their sacks of gold-dust with them. From one end of the deck to the other they could see no moving thing.

"What does it mean, Sir Daniel?" demanded Bill Bullock. "The boats were ashore. Does it mean Rogers and the rest are in the swamps seeking us? Maybe that's it, but I'll swear I saw someone wave from the deck up there, and —"

From somewhere in the depths of the ship came a muffled yell. Everyone stiffened. Everyone turned towards the bows.

It was then that the door under the poop-deck opened wide, and a score of men moved swiftly out, men with musketoons and steel breast-plates, men in the uniform of Spain.

"Stand where you are, Sir Daniel Darnby, unless you want to be massacred!" came a commanding voice. "We have you back and front."

The Laughing Pirate swung around to find his men covered by the twenty weapons. A whistle blew in the fore part of the ship, and the deck became alive with Spaniards who emerged from the hatches. The British crew was hemmed in on either side.

"A trap!" breathed Bill Bullock, and darted for one of the cannons on the starboard side.

Crash! A volley rang out from the muskets, and half a dozen British sailors fell. Bill Bullock dropped as lead hissed around him, and reached the gun on hands and knees. His effort was useless. The charge had been withdrawn. There was no time to load.

"Surrender!" repeated the tall, bearded Don who was in command. "It will serve you no purpose to be killed here and now, Sir Daniel. If you wish to save your men's lives, bid them lay down their weapons."

Sir Daniel's face was dark with fury. He knew the speaker. It was Don Lorenzo, of Santa Isabel, Governor of the port, entrusted with the shipping of the gold to Spain. The Laughing Pirate stuck his sword point downwards in the deck, and his men threw down their cutlasses, their pikes, and their pistols. It was one occasion when surrender was inevitable.

Don Lorenzo came swaggering forward, a mocking smile on his swarthy face. His men followed close behind, their weapons still levelled.

"It was good of you to deliver the gold so safely to me, Sir Daniel!" he said. "One of the guards of the mule-train escaped and took a short cut through the swamp to tell us what happened. I guessed you'd have a brig waiting for you somewhere on the coast, and made search for it. We surprised it last night, and have been waiting ever since. I am glad we do not have to wait longer. Now you will have the pleasure of sailing to Santa Isabel on your own ship. Your sword, Sir Daniel — hilt-first!"

He held out his hand commandingly. The Laughing Pirate reached for the sword-hilt, appeared to have some trouble in tugging it out of the woodwork, and bent it towards him. Then he let go with unexpected suddenness, and the spring of the finely tempered blade caused the upright sword to flash over the other way, catching Don Lorenzo in the stomach with terrific force.

The Spanish leader yelped with the pain of it, and clutched his stomach as he stepped back into the line of fire. The men with the muskets dared not fire, and Sir Daniel saw that.

With a quick jerk he had the sword in his hand, leapt to the side of the deck, ran through one Spaniard who tried to bar his way, and jumped on to the rail.

"I am not deserting ye, men!" he roared, then dived into the sea before a pistol or a firearm could be fired at him.

He struck the water heavily, and went underneath, diving immediately and scraping his back on the keel of the St. George.

Kicking out lustily, in spite of his muddy garments, he came up on the other side of the brig, grasped a rope, and hauled himself from the water.

It was all done so swiftly that the Spaniards had barely lined the opposite rail before he was clambering aboard behind their backs. Not a man saw him scramble over the low bulwarks and drop into the scuppers. Not a man saw him crawl towards the nearest hatch. They were too busy firing their muskets at shadows in the water, shouting excitedly that they could see the Laughing Pirate swimming under the surface.

The Laughing Pirate hastened down the gangway steps, hoping the trail of water he left behind would not be noticed in the excitement. He was breathing hard by the time he reached his own cabin, which showed signs of Don Lorenzo's occupancy.

He made for the bulkhead at the end, where hung the heavy cloak which he wore only in colder climes. Pulling this aside, he pressed a certain point, and two entire panels swung inwards. He peered inside, saw various kegs and boxes and grunted with satisfaction. Even though the Dons had searched the ship, they had not found his secret hiding-place.

He entered and closed the opening behind him. For the moment he was safe, still aboard his own ship, still armed.

A little later he heard the sound of stumbling feet, of blows, groans, and oaths. The noise descended into the hold. He guessed his men were being driven down below. The Spaniards had given them no time to resist. Their fate was settled. Some of them would be handed over to the Inquisition as heretics, while others, no less unfortunate, would be sold as slaves to the galleys or the plantations.

Not long afterwards the St. George got under way. She was putting to sea, heading for Santa Isabel.

Before long Don Lorenzo came down to the cabin, with another of his officers. The two talked over a flagon of wine, and although Don Lorenzo was overjoyed at the recapture of the gold, he was disappointed at the escape of Sir Daniel Darnby. He mentioned he had sent a messenger ashore for horsemen to scour the coast for the lone Englishman.

"I do not think he reached the shore," said the other Spaniard. "He dived deeply, and 'tis my opinion that he struck his head on a rock. I believe the English dog to be dead."

"Huh! Dead or not, we have his crew, his ship, and the gold. All Santa Isabel will turn out to do honour to us when we return," growled Don Lorenzo. "Waken me if anything exciting happens."

He loosened and removed his sword-belt and pistols, then stretched out on the Laughing Pirate's bunk and closed his eyes. The other officer went on deck.

The brig was moving sluggishly. There was very little wind. The day was a scorching hot one, with a sky like brass above. The Dons did not know how to get the best out of the St. George. The Laughing Pirate fidgetted and fretted in his stuffy refuge.

Through a knot-hole in the woodwork he could see the arrogant, upturned face of the sleeper. Don Lorenzo had tricked him once. Now was the time to return the compliment.

Quietly he opened the panel and slithered into the cabin. Dragging noises overhead told him the gold sacks were being hauled into one heap.

He tiptoed to the door, listened intently, found no one on the stairs, and returned to the cabin. It would have been easy to have run the Don through as he slept, but that was not Sir Daniel's intention. He contented himself with unloading both the man's pistols, then drew the keen Toledo blade from its ornamental scabbard.

His hands were slim, unusually white, and well kept, yet there was surprising strength in them. With no more than an appearance of effort, he bent the sword across his knee and snapped it in half. The lower, pointed end he pushed under the bunk, while the hilt and the foot-long upper section of the blade he returned to the scabbard.

Bending low, avoiding casting a shadow on the sleeper, he again made for the door.

Outside the steep ladderway led to the deck, but behind it was a narrow opening through which a man could squeeze to reach the long, narrow passage which ran the length of the ship. The Laughing Pirate plunged into this, sword in hand, keen eyes searching the shadows ahead. Only at the further end, under the forward hatch, was there much light.

In this way he came to the ladder which led down to the hold. The glimmer of a lantern told him someone was there. It was a Spanish soldier, sitting on top of the lower hatch, evidently guarding those in the hold.

Sir Daniel Darnby crept nearer. Voices came from below. Someone was begging for water for the wounded, who had been shut down there without any attention.

The Spanish soldier grinned evilly, and called:

"There is water in the bilge. Drink that!"

There was a movement behind him, and he tried to turn, but it was too late. The long, keen sword of the Laughing Pirate flashed across the shaft of lamp-light, and entered the fellow's scrawny throat. He gave a stifled screech, and fell backwards. For a few moments his limbs thrashed, then he lay still.

The Laughing Pirate dragged his body from the hatch and unbolted it. He lifted the lantern to shine it upon the upturned faces of the men below.

"'Tis me, my bullies!" he called softly. "Have a good heart. All will be well."

He called Bill Bullock up the ladder to him, and discussed a plan for re-taking the ship.

The mate of the St. George grunted with satisfaction, and passed down the sentry's wine-flask for the use of his injured comrades.

"Give us weapons, Sir Daniel, an' we'll do all you ask!" he vowed.

"I'll get the weapons," promised the Laughing Pirate, "but for the time being get ye below again. I must place the sentry over you."

The hatch closed, but not bolted, he propped the dead man against the nearest bulkhead so that anyone looking along the passageway from the other end would have seen the Spaniard sitting comfortably in the lamp-light, as though still on guard.

All this time the St. George was sailing southwards along the coast towards her destination. Santa Isabel was an important little port, well fortified, usually with a couple of big galleons as guard-ships. Many a time the Laughing Pirate had longed to get into that harbour in order to bombard the town, but had never before found a way of getting past the guard-ships. Now he believed he had found a way.

He made for the racks where cutlasses, muskets, and pikes were kept. Three times he made the trip, loading himself with weapons on each occasion. All these things, with powder and shot as well, he placed close beside the hatch from the hold, whispering down to his men to tell of his success.

"It won't be very long now," he said. "When you hear the first cannon fired, come on deck as fast as you can."

DON LORENZO had been wakened, and was buckling on his pistols and his sword-belt. Santa Isabel was in sight, and he tidied himself in readiness for a triumphant arrival.

A few minutes later he went on deck, and climbed up beside the Spanish flag, which had supplanted the flag of St. George. He had men with long trumpets waiting to give a fanfare.

No one saw the lone, crouching figure on the further side of the deck. The Laughing Pirate was loading one of his biggest cannons, which had previously been unloaded, like all the rest, by the Spaniards.

Twice he had to drop flat in the scuppers as a Spaniard hurried past. They were all discussing the feast which would be given in their honour when they got ashore.

So Sir Daniel Darnby waited as the ship drew nearer and nearer to the fortified entrance. On the inside the big galleons waited on either side. Then came a warning shot from a big gun, the heavy ball passing right over them. The Spaniards could not conceive it possible that such a small brig should dare to challenge them if it were a foe, but they were taking no chances.

No more shots were fired at them. The delighted garrison realised this was a vessel already captured by their astute Governor. They crowded on to the tops of the forts to cheer and wave as the gallant little St. George nosed gently inside. Flags were lowered in salute, and the cheering came clearly across the water.

Don Lorenzo postured on the poop-deck, drawn up to his full height, legs apart, hand on sword. He felt like a returning conqueror. It would be something to be known as the man who had deprived the notorious Laughing Pirate of his brig.

Under the guns of the forts they passed, between the two galleons, Almirante and Independecia, and the town lay before them, pink and gold in the late afternoon sunshine.

Behind the bulwarks on the starboard side Sir Daniel Darnby touched a glowing match to the vent in the loaded gun. Boo-oom! At that range it was impossible to miss. The heavy ball smashed squarely into the foot of the Almirante's main-mast, and brought it down with a tangle of riggings on her deck.

Yells of rage and surprise went up from the Spanish prize crew. They came swarming round the starboard side of the deck in time to see the Laughing Pirate entering the poop-house. He slammed the door behind him as they clustered forward.

Boom! Boom! Boom! Those on the Almirante had jumped to the conclusion they had been fooled. The firing of the cannon made them believe the St. George was not in the hands of their friends after all. They forthwith let fly at her with every gun they had on that side, forgetting she was too low in the water to suffer any hurt.

The cannon-balls whistled through the riggings and crashed aboard the Independecia, which promptly retaliated, believing the English brig was firing at her. For some four minutes the two galleons fought a duel with each other over the head of the St. George.

The firing of that first cannon had been the signal for the British sailors in the hold. They heaved the hatch upwards, rolling the dead Spaniard aside. They seized the weapons which had been placed there for them, and raced for the deck.

Crashing noises told that attempts were being made to batter down the door of Sir Daniel's refuge. He was yelling defiance from the other side. Everyone was so intent on this that they did not see the English sailors, led by Bill Bullock, until it was too late.

Cold steel and cutlasses were the order of the day, and the English sailors cut a way through to the door almost quicker than it takes to tell. It was then the door was flung open, and the Laughing Pirate appeared, eyes sparkling with delight as he hurled himself into the fray.

The Spaniards split up and fled to various parts of the brig, which was by this time in the middle of the harbour. Both the galleons were on fire. Nothing was being fired at the St. George, but one of the forts was firing blindly out to sea, evidently believing more English ships were coming in.

"Bombard the town! Land some balls in those barracks! Let the Dons know they're not safe from us even here!" roared Sir Daniel, and turned when he heard an angry shout.

"English dog!" snarled Don Lorenzo, jerking up a pistol and pulling trigger at point-blank range.

There was a click, but nothing more. Sir Daniel had done well to unload. The angry Don snatched the other pistol out and tried the same thing, with like result. Choking with passion, he whipped his sword from its scabbard, and discovered he had less than half a blade.

The next moment there was a sword-point at his throat, and the Laughing Pirate advised:

"Better surrender, Don Lorenzo! You will have no other chance."

The man rolled his eyes, frothed at the mouth, then admitted his defeat. Sir Daniel shouted the news to the other Spaniards that their leader had surrendered. They were only too glad to throw down their arms before the British cutlasses could get at them.

With Bill Bullock at the wheel, the St. George came round as gracefully as a swan. All was panic and confusion in the harbour. The shore guns were not even manned. Smaller crafts raced each other across the waterfront. There was panic in the military barracks as the first two cannon-balls from the St George crashed through the adobe walls.

Nobody quite knew what had happened. It seemed incredible that a pirate ship could have got past the defences, but here it was, spitting ball after ball into the barracks and the town, starting considerable fires which added to the volume of the smoke cloud.

Sir Daniel knew he dared not wait there long. He did as much damage as he could in five minutes, then headed for the narrow exit with all sails set, guns silent, his men crouching at their posts.

The burning galleons supplied them with a smoke-screen and when they suddenly appeared through this, right between the two forts, the gunners ashore were too surprised to fire. Not so those on the St. George. Boom! Boom! Boom! Their cannons thundered on either side, and the forts received a severe pasting before the rolling smoke again hid the venturesome "prize" which had dared to bombard those who had captured it.

Once through the gap the brig showed a clean pair of heels, With the coming of evening a strong breeze always came up, and they scudded along in a northerly direction, knowing that darkness would soon protect them from any pursuers.

As a matter of fact, owing to the damage and confusion caused in the port of Santa Isabel, no vessel ever put to sea in chase of them. The Dons were too busy arguing as to whose fault this sorry affair really was.

Those men who had fought their way through the swamps with sacks of gold, now not only found themselves safely aboard their own vessel, but in possession of numerous prisoners, and with the satisfaction of knowing they had penetrated one of the best-defended harbours on the Spanish Main.

Late that night, some twenty miles from Santa Isabel, the St. George lay to, and a boat was dropped over-side. Into it the Spanish prisoners and their leader were told to climb. They were being given a chance to gain the shore and return to their battered township.

The Laughing Pirate handed down Don Lorenzo, grinning broadly as he said:

"Adios, Don Lorenzo! I hope you have enjoyed your little trip aboard my humble brig. If I had more room to spare I would take you on a longer voyage, but the gold takes up so much space I have little for passengers . . . It was nice of you to give me the chance to visit Santa Isabel. It is an honour I have looked forward to for some years."

The Don snarled, the released Spaniards dipped their oars, and the boat sped away from the saucy brig which had proved such an expensive prize to those who had captured her for such a short time.

---

**From a great adventure to some small ADventures ... another selection of weird and wonderful adverts from years gone by.**

---

---

# THE WOLF OF KABUL

OF all the British outposts along the North-West Frontier of India, there was none so smart and spotless as Fort Kanda, which stood right at the east end of the Khyber Pass.

The flag that flew on the fort was always perfectly clean. The floors of the fort were scrubbed every day. There was not a single rifle in the fort with a speck of rust on it, and even the pots in the cook-house were polished like mirrors. The man in charge of the fort was Colonel Laurie.

One day into this perfect fort strolled a man who looked like a tramp.

This newcomer had flopped off a skinny mule, then strolled up to the sentry at the gates with his hands thrust deep into his pockets and a battered sun-helmet stuck on the back of his head.

"Hullo," he said cheerfully. "I'm Bill Samson — where's the Colonel?"

The sentry looked the ragged figure up and down, then with a snort pointed the way to the Colonel's quarters, and the strange figure ambled into the fort.

He paused a few yards away, fumbled in his pocket, and produced an old briar pipe. He stuffed it with tobacco and, lighting up, tossed the lighted match on the spotless parade ground.

"Blimey!" spluttered a Cockney solider, peeping out of the guardhouse. "The Colonel will half murder him for that. Who is the cove, anyway?"

"That's the famous Bill Samson," said an older soldier, who had been on the Frontier for some years. "His real job is surveying the Frontier and making maps of the mountains and passes, but he knows the native languages and customs so well that he always gets the job of busting up any trouble among the Afghan and Pathan tribes. The natives call him the Wolf of Kabul."

Bill Samson was at that moment sauntering into the office of Colonel Laurie. The Colonel gaped at the sight of his visitor.

"I believe you sent a message to headquarters saying that two tribes up here are getting dangerous," the Wolf said.

"Yes, I did," the officer replied shortly. "What about it?"

"I've been sent here to put a damper on those tribes," Bill Samson returned calmly. "That's all!"

The Colonel could only stare. His fort was threatened by a native rising. He had asked for help, and headquarters had sent this lone tramp!

"Shir Muhammud and Gunga Khan have joined forces and declared a holy war, isn't that right?" went on the visitor. "Their troops are in the mountains just west of here, and they intend to wipe Fort Kanda off the map as their first move. These two chiefs have been harmless up to now, because they've always been fighting against each other. Now they have joined, and have become a danger. That's right, isn't it?"

"It is," was the stiff answer. "The two chiefs have sworn blood-brotherhood and are gathering their men. The combined tribes are about ten thousand strong."

After his reply Colonel Laurie gave his moustache a fierce twirl. His hands were itching to take a grip on this young fellow and hurl him out of the room.

But the Colonel knew something of Bill Samson's history. Bill had not been nicknamed the Wolf of Kabul for nothing. Bill wasn't an army man, but he was the most useful man in India to the army.

Pompous officials hated him because he had no respect for their dignity. The lower ranks adored him because he openly preferred their company.

Just then there was a tap on the door of the outer office. A Sepoy entered, one of the native soldiers of the British Army in India.

"Private Chung is in trouble again, sir," he said.

"Fetch him in!" barked the Colonel, going to his desk.

There entered three Sepoys with fixed bayonets. A native sergeant swaggered at the head of them and the prisoner came along in the rear.

Fort Kanda's commander groaned with despair as he looked at the prisoner. Chung was the black sheep in that otherwise perfect fort.

He was a squat man with enormous shoulders and very long arms. His ugly face was broad and flat, with greasy, black hair hanging over his forehead. He was dressed in the uniform of a Sepoy private, but there was no smartness about his uniform.

Chung was a mountain man from the Eastern Himalayas.

"Lord," he said, his beady eyes filled with sadness. "I am full of humble sorrow. I did not mean to knock down four men. Lord, the clicky-ba merely turned in my hand!"

"What is the charge — and what is a 'clicky-ba'?" demanded the Colonel, looking at the native sergeant.

"Sahib, a 'clicky-ba' is what this ignorant fellow calls a cricket bat. It was with one he did the damage which placed four men in the hospital. Sahib, he is very bad."

"Read the charge," ordered the Colonel.

The sergeant did so. It said that while being taught the game of cricket, Private Chung had been stumped, but he refused to leave his wicket. On an attempt being made to remove him, he had used the bat as a club and cracked the heads of four of the fielders. He had then wept bitterly and been easily disarmed.

"Truly it is as the sergeant says," sighed the prisoner. "It was strange what the clicky-ba did. I would like always to be armed with such a weapon. Lord, will you give me a clicky-ba instead of a rifle?"

"I'll give you a week in the cells and then you'll be kicked out of the army!" roared the Colonel. "Take him away!"

"I hope sweet perfumes will always be in your nostrils," murmured Chung humbly as he was marched out.

Colonel Laurie groaned and, turning swiftly, found Bill Samson at his elbow.

"I like that man Chung," Bill said. "I want a servant like that — a born fighter. I'll take him over to Afghanistan and end this little affair we were talking about."

"Take Chung?" cried the Colonel. "He'd knife you."

"No he wouldn't. I know that type," said the young fellow cheerfully, then became suddenly grave. "Listen," he went on, "there are plenty of spies who know I've come up here, so I'm going right back to headquarters, and I'll slip into native disguise. I'm going to the mountains to join Shir Muhammud, and I'll stir up more trouble for those people than you can guess."

He tapped the surprised officer on the chest in a familiar manner.

"I shall come back to the fort in a few hours. I shall be disguised as a native. I'll insult one of your sentries, and you must lock me up in the cells with Chung. Tonight you will allow Chung and I to escape. The Afghan spies will learn all about that escape, and we'll be received with open arms by the tribesmen, and I shan't be suspected for who I am."

With these words Bill Samson stalked out. A few minutes later his mule was plodding away from Fort Kanda.

Bill Samson returned to Fort Kanda late in the afternoon. He was disguised as a fierce hillman. At the gates he kicked the sentry and was arrested after a struggle and taken to the cells. He was put in the same cell as Chung.

Nobody else but the colonel was in on the secret. The whole affair was for the purpose of fooling any spies who might be about.

Before sunrise, however, the bugles were blowing the alarm, for the Sepoy guarding the cells was found neatly trussed with his own turban-cloth, and Chung and the disguised Bill Samson were missing.

So was a very fine cricket bat belonging to Colonel Laurie, also a silver tea-set much prized by the Colonel's wife.

The cricket bat was being twirled between the stumpy fingers of Chung as he strode happily through the hills by the side of Bill Samson.

"Will there be use for Clicky-ba where we go, lord?" asked Chung.

"Much use," said Bill Samson shortly. "We go to Kohi, the city of rebellion."

They were rapidly approaching the Afghan frontier, where a row of coloured posts marked the limits of British India. Suddenly Bill Samson halted and looked back. An army mule patrol was hot on their heels.

It had been sent out by Colonel Laurie, who had decided that Bill Samson had gone quite beyond the score when he had pinched Mrs Laurie's tea-set.

Then a flash came from amongst the rocks on the Afghan side of the line. Bill Samson grinned. They were being watched by tribesmen. The gleam came from the sun striking a rifle barrel. "This will help a lot," he muttered, and then he turned to Chung. "You shall use Clicky-ba to send away these foolish Sepoys who are following us," he said.

"Lord, it shall be a joy," said the grinning hillman cheerfully.

He dropped out of sight amongst the rocks and the Britisher hurried on to the Frontier. The patrol, which was under the same native sergeant as had accused Chung before the Colonel, charged down towards the Frontier line.

Then with a terrible yell Chung sprang out of his ambush.

The brightly-varnished cricket bat rose and fell with a dull thud on a man's head, sending him sprawling. Another Sepoy was sent down with a back sweep. Chung crooned a little song as he aimed mighty swipes, but he was careful to use only a part of his enormous strength. He did not want to kill the Sepoys.

The sight of his old enemy, the sergeant, angered him a little however. The Sepoy advanced on Chung with fixed bayonet, but a single sweep of Clicky-ba knocked the weapon out of the sergeant's hands. The man turned to jump clear. But Chung scored a boundary hit on the seat of his military shorts, lifting him a yard into the air. The rout of that native patrol was complete.

Chung came racing between the rocks. He reached his master and stood before him very humbly, leaning on the handle of the bat.

"Lord, I am full of sorrow. Truly, I did not intend to make it unpleasant for the sergeant to sit down. I swear the Clicky-ba turned in my hand and did this evil thing."

"Call me not Lord," cut in Bill Samson. "I am Ali. Remember my real name means death to us both."

They crossed the Frontier line, and soon they were climbing a narrow pass leading to the desert and the town of Kohi, which was the headquarters of the rebellious chiefs. As they rounded a large rock halfway up the pass, a number of wild hillmen rose silently on either side of them and menaced them with rifles.

They were the Afghans Bill Samson had known to be watching when Chung was fighting the patrol.

"Where do you go?" they asked.

"To Kohi and the noble Shir Muhammud," the disguised Bill Samson replied. "We would fight in his holy war, for, by Allah! — we hate these British dogs. We have just escaped from the prison of Fort Kanda."

"It is true that two men were imprisoned there and escaped," nodded the Afghan leader. "What proof have you that you are these ones?"

Bill Samson laughed as he emptied the contents of a sack on the ground. Out rolled the silver tea-set of the Colonel's wife.

"Of a truth you are the ones we expected," nodded the leader.

"Where is Shir Muhammud?" Bill Samson demanded. "I go to join him. I do not care for that fox Gunga Khan — I would as soon fight him as fight the British."

The Afghans muttered in their beards, for they were all Gunga Khan's men and hated Shir Muhammud like poison.

The fact that they took it quietly and helped the pair on their way to Kohi showed the danger that lurked at the gates of Fort Kanda. The rival chiefs had joined together in a holy war, forgetting their enmity for the time being.

When the Wolf and Chung entered the little hill town of Kohi at sundown, they found it packed with thousands of armed warriors.

The Wolf came to the courtyard where Shir Muhammud squatted on a pile of carpets and stroked his long beard. From time to time the great chief looked round suspiciously at his old rival Gunga Khan, who occupied another divan by his side.

The two chiefs hated each other, and for ten years they had fought each other, until they had joined their forces to sweep the British off the Frontier. They could not, however, forget the past.

Bill Samson caused some more ill-feeling when he marched in and laid the silver tea-set at the foot of Shir Muhammud.

"I took them from Fort Kanda as a present for you, lord," he said gaily. "By Allah, I will fight for you — I and my brother. We are your men."

And he turned his back on Gunga Khan with such open disgust that the Afghan shook with rage. Shir Muhammud stroked his beard and chuckled.

"Stand behind me," he said. "I give you my blessing."

There was a gasp of fury from the rival chief seated on the other divan.

It seemed as if Bill Samson had acted like a madman in making an enemy of Gunga Khan, the other chieftain. Even Shir Muhammud advised him in a whisper to keep to the palace and not leave it until they marched on Fort Kanda.

"Nay, lord, I am not afraid of that fox or his sleepy dogs," Bill sneered. "My brother and I, we are good enough for all of them."

As for Gunga Khan, he was so angry that he quarrelled with Shir Muhammud and then swept away with his followers to another part of the town. Shir Muhammud went away with his chieftains, and Bill Samson and Chung were left alone.

Kohi was a town of winding alleys sheltered by high, white walls. There were no lights, and when the Wolf and Chung went out into the streets they stumbled over the holes dug in the ground to serve as drains.

Soon they reached a narrow street leading to the bazaar, where many fierce hillmen chanted songs of battle. Bill Samson promptly broke in with a famous hill tune, which was the battle song of Shir Muhammud.

He was still singing when the fun began.

A party of Gunga Khan's followers, forgetting the vows of peace laid down by the priests, took their knives and silently drifted away from the bazaar. It was time the insolent stranger was put out of the way.

Coming round a bend leading into a dark square, Bill Samson and Chung walked right into them.

A huge, bearded hillman seized the Wolf by the front of his robe. "Dog," he hissed, "we have had too much of your insolence. Tonight you praise Gunga Khan, or you die. Say this — 'Gunga Khan, lord of the hills, greatest of chiefs.' Now hasten, for my knife thirsts for thy blood."

He held the long blade to Bill Samson's throat, yet the reply was a short laugh.

"Gunga Khan, the old hill fox in his burrow!" said the Wolf.

His fist shot up at the same time catching the giant on the beard and cracking his jaw. Snatching his deadly daggers from his sash, Bill Samson crouched and faced the howling pack.

With howls of rage Gunga Khan's followers closed in, but two of them were down before they knew what had hit them. They lay senseless on the ground with crushed skulls. The terrible Chung and his cricket bat were in action.

The hillman was mad with the lust for battle. There was a foam on his thick lips, and his beady eyes had a red gleam.

The knives Bill held himself were red to the hilts, and not a rival thrust had reached beyond them. Not for nothing was Bill Samson known as the Wolf of Kabul, and his fangs were his gleaming knives. Finally the Afghans turned and fled, terror-stricken.

"Lord," said Chung, looking at the dead tribesmen, "this is a very terrible thing. I am all sadness. Truly Clicky-ba turned in my hand and I knew not what it did. By the light of the Buddha I swear I did not intend to kill. Lord, I killed at least fifteen and I am humbly sorry."

The mad look came back as he shook the hair from his eyes and glared round. Just then two parties of Afghans burst into the square from either side, and another terrible fight began.

The Britisher and his servant had landed in Gunga Khan's section of Kohi, so there was nobody to help them.

A fierce band of screaming men surged round the Wolf and Chung. Chung was bleeding from many wounds, but fought all the harder. The Britisher had lost a dagger, thrust deeply into the throat of one of the attackers.

Of course, that great defence could not last, for more and more of Gunga Khan's men were arriving. A terrible sweep from a heavy scimitar crashed through Bill Samson's guard, and the broad of the blade landed on his head, sending him senseless to the ground.

Immediately Chung jumped across his master's body, his screams and wolf-like howls striking terror into the hearts of the Afghans. They got him at last, however, with a huge sheet which they flung over him and Clicky-ba. Twelve men struggled to hold him down, but it took them all their time, such was his terrible strength.

Bill Samson, dangling limp and senseless, was carried in the arms of a single hillman. It was startling to think that this young fellow, so slight in build, had killed ten men and wounded a dozen more.

As for Chung, they put ropes on him and dragged him along like a mad bull. He still roared defiantly, and fought to free himself.

One of Gunga Khan's men had gone ahead to warn his master. The chieftain rubbed his hands with glee when he heard that the stranger who had openly insulted him in the presence of Shir Muhammud had been caught.

So Bill Samson and Chung were taken to the courtyard of a small mosque. The Afghans flung the Britisher down on the flagstones inside the mosque, and tied Chung to a pillar for safety. Then Gunga Khan appeared.

The Afghan clapped his hands, and men came in, dragging a big block of wood, with a huge, sharp spike about two feet long sticking up in the middle.

At a signal from Gunga Khan, four big natives, naked to the waist, grabbed Bill Samson by the wrists and ankles, swinging him spread-eagled over that dreadful spike. When the moment came they would bring him down with such

force that the point would drive into his back and through his chest. The Wolf was now conscious, but dazed.

Already Gunga Khan had lifted his hand, when Chung, with a terrible yell, broke the ropes which held him to the pillar as if they were threads.

Snatching Clicky-ba from a man who held it, Chung flung himself on the Afghans, cracking skulls right and left. One man he seized by the beard, and, exerting his enormous strength, swung him off his feet and flung him like a stone at the men who held the Wolf.

The executioners were knocked off balance, carrying Bill Samson away from the dreaded spike. Seeing Chung coming for them the executioners dropped the Wolf and ran for their lives, but even their speed did not save them. Chung heaved up the spiked block and flung it after them, crushing two beneath that great weight.

The mighty Himalayan screamed as he stood over Bill Samson and dropped men left and right with mighty swipes of Clicky-ba. The Afghans retreated.

Stooping swiftly, Chung swung his master over his broad shoulders and whirling the bat plunged into the crowd.

"Kill them!" screamed Gunga Khan, shaking with fury.

The Afghans couldn't stop Chung although they tried. He brushed aside knives carelessly and plunged into the cool interior of the mosque, dropping his burden and turning to defend the door with Clicky-ba.

It was at that moment Bill Samson recovered and sat up.

The sight of his strange servant fighting an army cleared his brain.

He scrambled up and looked round for some sort of weapon.

Piled in one corner were a number of cases. One was partly opened, and he saw the barrel of a machine-gun. Gunga Khan had been storing arms that had been smuggled into the country.

"Keep them out, Chung!" yelled Bill Samson as he began to set up the machine-gun.

Chung still fought with the same fury, pausing occasionally to shake the greasy hair from his eyes. When Bill Samson had a belt of cartridges fitted he called for Chung to jump clear, but it was more than a minute before Chung obeyed. The Afghans, urged on by Gunga Khan, rushed forward.

"I can hold them!" called Bill Samson. "Chung, you will do as I say. Leave the mosque by the back door and run to Shir Muhammud. Tell him how we were attacked by the men of Gunga Khan and sentenced to death without trial. Tell him that I beg help."

For a moment Chung hesitated, fingering Clicky-ba and dreaming of more slaughter. His master, however, shot him a quick look from his cold blue eyes.

"Go!" he commanded.

"Lord, I obey; but if you are dead when I come back I will kill every man in Kohi!"

He vanished swiftly. The door his master had pointed out was securely locked, so he dragged the iron grid from a window, flung it at the crowds going down before the machine-gun, and dropped out into the lane.

Meanwhile Bill Samson had cleared

the courtyard, and contented himself with sharp-shooting. The Afghans had gone to cover, and were bringing their own rifles into play. The Britisher had to heave a crate by the side of his weapon and crouch down behind it.

Of course, he would not be able to keep the Afghans at bay for ever, and it was touch and go if the other chieftain would come.

But he had judged his man well, and when Shir Muhammud heard the wild story from the lips of the still wilder Chung, he fairly flamed with rage. He remembered the silver tea-set presented to him.

"By Allah, that fox Gunga Khan has gone too far!" he roared. "No man of mine shall die at the stake."

He clapped his hands, and in a few minutes his men were preparing for battle. The holy war of the mullahs was forgotten, and the British could do as they pleased. The lust for the blood of Gunga Khan and his followers was even stronger.

So presently it came about that several thousand screaming natives swept down on the mosque, waving guns and knives, and shouting insults against Gunga Khan.

Promptly the Afghan chief turned out his men and a terrible fight between the two tribes began in the narrow streets. Bill Samson found himself alone in the mosque, and he chuckled as he heard the uproar. His mission to Kohi was at an end.

The Wolf found a rifle amongst the cases of arms and went out to look for Chung. A squat figure loomed up and stood panting by his side.

"Lord," said Chung very sorrowfully, "I am humble, I ask your forgiveness, for truly I knew not what happened. There was a fight and Clicky-ba moved in my hand and killed many men on the way here. Lord, it is a very terrible thing to kill men."

"We will find two fast mules and hasten over the Frontier. My work is done," said the Wolf.

When the troops at Fort Kanda were parading in the early morning, Bill Samson and Chung sauntered through the gates, looking like tramps in their blood-stained, torn, and dirty robes. It took Colonel Laurie some minutes to recognise Bill Samson.

"Confound you!" he roared. "What d'you mean by stealing my wife's tea-set and treating the patrol like that?"

Bill Samson spat deliberately on the spotless parade ground and his blue eyes flickered slightly.

"Send a chit down to Nushki for a tea-set," he said. "You'll get a new one there. Your set helped to stop a Frontier rising! Gunga Khan and Shir Muhammud have started a feud that will last for a hundred years."

"And Clicky-ba has killed a thousand men," boasted Chung, staring challengingly at his old enemy, the sergeant. "Ho, in my hand it turned and did many evil things for which I weep."

"But — but —" choked Colonel Laurie. "Do you mean to say Fort Kanda isn't any longer in danger?"

"Not a bit," said Bill Samson.

And he sauntered out with Chung at his heels. The Wolf of Kabul had done his work.

The Wolf Of Kabul and Chung continued their adventures in the pages of HOTSPUR. This story dates from 1961.

Chung and his master were always on the lookout for unrest among the fiery native chiefs. One day, in the frontier town of Elabad, they found trouble brewing.

THAT'S THE MAD MULLAH. HE IS TRYING TO STIR UP THE TRIBESMEN INTO A WAR WITH THE BRITISH. WE MUST STOP HIM, CHUNG.

They followed the Mullah.

NOW'S OUR CHANCE. COME ON, CHUNG.

QUICK! CHUNG. I'LL TAKE HIS CLOTHES. YOU TIE HIM UP.

HIDE THE MULLAH IN THE CELLAR. I'M GOING TO MAKE ANOTHER SPEECH TO THE TRIBESMEN IN HIS PLACE. WE LOOK ALIKE.

And so —

— AND SO, MY BROTHERS, WAR COSTS MONEY. I NEED FUNDS TO BUY WEAPONS TO BEAT THE BRITISH. GIVE ME ALL THE MONEY AND JEWELS YOU HAVE.

THE TRIBAL CHIEFS ARE RICH.

BRING THE CHEST IN HERE. THEN STAND GUARD ON THE DOOR.

That night.

GOOD. THE TWO SENTRIES HAVE SEEN US SNEAKING OFF.

THERE'S THE MULLAH.

Next morning.

THE MULLAH HAS STOLEN OUR MONEY! AFTER HIM! HE WAS CARRYING A BAG WHEN WE SAW HIM LAST NIGHT!

WE'VE DRAWN THEM WELL AWAY FROM THE TOWN NOW. GIVE THEM BACK THEIR TREASURE, CHUNG.

YES, LORD!

THEY WILL FIGHT EACH OTHER FOR THE LOOT. THAT IS THEIR FINE FOR MAKING WAR ON THE BRITISH.

WE WILL FIGHT TOO, LORD. CLICKY BA WILL CRUSH SKULLS.

CLICKY BA TURNS IN MY HANDS. I SMELL BLOOD!

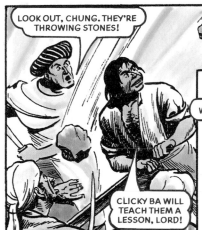

LOOK OUT, CHUNG. THEY'RE THROWING STONES!

CLICKY BA WILL TEACH THEM A LESSON, LORD!

A BOUNDARY HIT, O LORD!

WELL HIT, CHUNG!

AAGH!

QUICK, CHUNG! ALONG THAT LEDGE THEN BACK TO THE TOWN.

Back in Elabad.

WE'LL GO AND RELEASE THE MULLAH, NOW!

THE WAYS OF THE WOLF ARE STRANGE.

CUT THE MULLAH FREE AND GIVE HIM BACK HIS CLOTHES.

YES, LORD! BUT I WOULD RATHER CRACK HIS SKULL!

When the real Mullah appeared, the tribesmen chased him.

THERE HE IS! KILL HIM! HE STOLE OUR MONEY!

NOW YOU SEE MY IDEA IN FREEING THE MULLAH, CHUNG. HE WILL NEVER STIR UP TROUBLE AGAIN!

TRULY, LORD, YOU ARE WELL-NAMED THE WOLF. YOU ARE VERY CUNNING, INDEED.

THAT'S THE MULLAH TAKEN CARE OF, CHUNG. BUT THERE'S ALWAYS WORK FOR US ON THE FRONTIER.

YES, LORD, AND MANY SKULLS TO CRACK!

The Wolf of Kabul and Chung were called to a meeting with Colonel Scott, to be given their next mission.

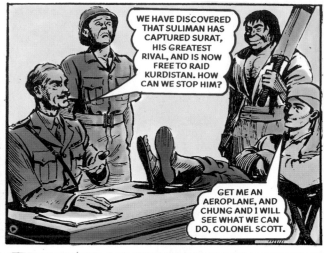

WE HAVE DISCOVERED THAT SULIMAN HAS CAPTURED SURAT, HIS GREATEST RIVAL, AND IS NOW FREE TO RAID KURDISTAN. HOW CAN WE STOP HIM?

GET ME AN AEROPLANE, AND CHUNG AND I WILL SEE WHAT WE CAN DO, COLONEL SCOTT.

WHO IS THAT DIRTY-LOOKING CHARACTER, SIR?

THAT'S BILL SAMSON, THE WOLF OF KABUL. HE'S THE BEST BRITISH AGENT ON THE FRONTIER.

Later, in the hills —

COME BACK FOR US AT DAWN IN THREE DAYS' TIME.

RIGHTO!

Wolf and Chung reached the mountain hide-out of Surat, the bandit leader, who had been captured by Suliman.

NOW SURAT IS A PRISONER, I'LL BET THESE TWO ARE FIGHTING FOR LEADERSHIP OF THE BANDITS.

I, NADIR, AM LEADER NOW. WHO DARES TO CHALLENGE ME?

YOU ARE A BOASTER, NADIR. I, ALI, CHALLENGE YOU!

MY MASTER HAS KILLED THOUSANDS OF MEN!

WHAT A FIGHTER! ALI SHALL BE OUR LEADER.

FOLLOW ME! WE ARE GOING TO RESCUE SURAT!

HURRAH!

AND CLICKY BA WILL CRACK MORE SKULLS.

Then, outside Suliman's village —

WE'RE JUST IN TIME. SULIMAN'S GOING TO HANG SURAT, BUT THOSE CATTLE GIVE ME AN IDEA FOR RESCUING HIM.

In a desolate mountain pass The Wolf and Chung encountered a staggering figure.

LOOK, CHUNG! A WOUNDED BRITISH OFFICER — WITH AFRIDI TRIBESMEN AFTER HIM!

CLICKY BA TURNS IN MY HANDS, LORD! I WILL CRACK MANY SKULLS!

I'M BILL SAMSON, THE WOLF OF KABUL. WHAT'S HAPPENED?

AFRIDIS — CAPTURED COLONEL BRYANT — HE'S WOUNDED — MUST RESCUE —

THAT OFFICER WAS A BRAVE MAN. WE MUST GET HELP TO BRYANT. THERE'S AN INDIAN DOCTOR IN A NEARBY VILLAGE. I WONDER . . .

I HOPE THIS DOCTOR'S DISGUISE FOOLS THE AFRIDI SENTRY.

HALT! WHAT DO YOU WANT?

Several hours later Wolf and Chung approached the Afridi camp.

IF YOU ARE A DOCTOR YOU ARE JUST THE MAN MY MASTER WANTS. WE HAVE A WOUNDED SAHIB. GO INTO THE CAMP.

I AM ILHOM KHAN, CHIEF OF THE AFRIDI . . . CURE THIS MAN. IF HE DIES, YOU DIE TOO.

I'M THE WOLF OF KABUL. I'VE COME TO GET YOU OUT OF HERE. FIRST, I'LL HAVE TO DAB THIS BLUE LOTION ON YOU.

THE HIGHLY SEASONED FOOD THEY EAT MAKES THEM DRINK A LOT. HE WILL SOON FEEL ILL.

HE WILL BE ALL RIGHT SOON, BUT HE HAS A FEVER AND MUST NOT BE DISTURBED.

VERY WELL. NOW YOU WILL EAT WITH US.

I'LL SLIP THIS PILL INTO THE WATER BAG. ILHOM KHAN IS NEXT TO DRINK.

AT SCHOOL IN 1975

In 1937, this was *HOTSPUR'S* idea of a school four decades on. Take a close look at the boys' ski-pants style trousers. We don't recall seeing many pairs like that back in '75.

Football a thing of the past? Hard to believe, but according to this story from *WIZARD* in 1948 that will be the case by the year 2148.

THERE WAS ONCE A GAME CALLED FOOTBALL

V.E.3.

THE END OF THE WORLD

Let's hope that this scene from *ROVER* will always remain in the realms of fiction.

ADVENTURE

OCT. 5TH 1940 No. 988

THE AMAZING STORY OF LIFE AS IT WILL BE IN THE YEAR 2040! READ—"WARDENS OF THE WORLDS IN SPACE"

The editor of *ADVENTURE* in 1940 reckoned that astronauts a hundred years from then would be wearing goldfish bowls and riding boots, while patrolling the Milky Way. Fifty years later we can safely say he was wide of the mark.